The Blue Flames That Keep Us Warm

THE BLUE FLAMES
THAT KEEP US WARM

Mike McCardell's Favourite Stories

Mike McCardell

HARBOUR PUBLISHING

Harbour Publishing Co. Ltd.
P.O. Box 219
Madeira Park, BC
V0N 2H0
www.harbourpublishing.com

Printed and bound in Canada

THE CANADA COUNCIL | LE CONSEIL DES ARTS
FOR THE ARTS | DU CANADA
SINCE 1957 | DEPUIS 1957

BRITISH
COLUMBIA
ARTS COUNCIL
Supported by the Province of British Columbia

Harbour Publishing acknowledges financial support from the Government
of Canada through the Book Publishing Industry Development Program
and the Canada Council for the Arts, and from the Province of British
Columbia through the British Columbia Arts Council and the Book
Publisher's Tax Credit through the Ministry of Provincial Revenue.

Library and Archives Canada Cataloguing in Publication

McCardell, Mike, 1944–
    The blue flames that keep us warm : Mike McCardell's favourite
stories.

ISBN 978-1-55017-440-3

    1. British Columbia—Anecdotes. 2. British Columbia—Miscellanea.
3. McCardell, Mike, 1944– I. Title.
FC3847.36.M442 2007   C818'.602   C2007-904200-7

Dear Ruby

You are now the story god

Contents

Blue Flames

When I was in the third grade I was taken on a field trip at Public School 54, which is in New York City.

My mother had just left my father, a feat she accomplished in the middle of the night while he was lying drunk on the floor in the hallway of our apartment. He had some issues.

She'd woken me up and, with a finger against her lips, said, "Ssshhh. We're going." She must have been very brave.

We left while it was still dark and cold. She carried a suitcase. I had a coat over my pajamas. We took a bus, then a subway, and rode for almost an hour, getting off in another part of the city where my mother's sister lived. It was the longest trip I had ever taken.

By the time we got to my aunt's house, the sun was up, and I could see my cousin, who was four years older than me, sweeping the front steps. I thought this was a very grown-up thing to do. I had never seen anyone sweep outside before.

To make room for my mother and me, he slept in the hallway, which I know his parents hated, but he loved.

I transferred to P.S. 54, the same school he went to. I was afraid of the third grade because my cousin told me I would have to do long division. I did not know how to do division.

Sometime during that year my class was told we were going on a field trip and we did not need our coats. The teacher led us out of the classroom, then down the stairs to the school basement, then down a set of metal stairs to the boiler room below and a huge furnace.

Our teacher introduced us to the school custodian. All of us already knew him as the man who swept the hallways.

The custodian told us to gather around the furnace, from which we could feel the heat, and then he opened the grating and we saw a long oval of flames. He said they were dancing blue fires that were keeping us warm. Then he closed the grating and we went back up to the classroom.

More than half a century later my wife and I were babysitting our granddaughter in Vancouver, which is on the other side of the continent from P.S. 54. I was outside sweeping the front steps with the help of my granddaughter when my wife complained that the house was cold. I went down to check the furnace. It was out. I got some matches from the kitchen and called my granddaughter, who was almost three, to come with me downstairs.

I opened the metal grating on the front of the furnace and lit a match. Then I turned on the pilot light, and a minute later a long oval of flames jumped up. I told my granddaughter those were the dancing blue flames that were keeping us warm.

She stared at them for a while, then said, "Now can we have ice cream?"

Some day, if they still have natural gas, she may light a fire for some other kid, possibly her granddaughter, who I will never know. And she will say, those are the dancing blue flames that are keeping us warm. She may add, "Once upon a time my grandfather told me that. Now let's get some ice cream."

There is nothing better in life, besides breathing, love, kindness and laughing, than small stories with warm endings.

The stories in this book are mostly from television tales I have done. They are like little blue flames. Sometimes they can burn fingers, but mostly they keep us warm. And they go well with a bowl of ice cream, especially chocolate.

These stories exist for me forever as they were when I found them. Although everyone grows old and moves aside for the next inhabitants of their square foot of land, most of the characters in this book are still alive. The last time I checked, the submarine was still on the balcony in New Westminster and Trout Lake still had kids fishing on it.

The First is Last

It says so in the Bible. The last shall come first and the first last. I don't know why, but I think the Bible writers were predicting a certain day in Vancouver when the Shriners came to town.

Why was I going to do a story on the Shriners? Well, because they are an incredibly good group who do amazing and wonderful things for kids who are hurting. That was reason enough. And also because they were having their international convention in town. Of course I would do a story on them. Do you think I was going to spend a desperate day looking for a sweet kid splashing in a puddle when there were ten thousand men wearing funny hats walking around town? I would take the easy way out.

But mostly I was going to do a story because Allison Hollingsworth, who was Tony Parsons's private secretary and has been married to a Shriner for longer than Grouse has been a mountain, kept asking me, "Are you going to do a story on the Shriners?"

"Yes," I told her.

The next day she reminded me.

"I won't forget," I said.

The following day she told me the Shriners were coming to town.

"I know, I'm doing a story about them."

"That's nice," she said. "Because I would hate to think I was influencing you."

A few days before they arrived, she told me she was taking some time off work to help prepare for the visit of the Shriners. Did I know they were having a parade, and could she tell them it would be on television?

"A good thing you reminded me," I told her.

And then came the day and we were at the parade, which in a few minutes would be going along Pacific Boulevard, and there were thousands of people standing on the sidewalk watching grown men with fezzes on their heads riding tiny motorcycles in circles.

And there were clowns, any of who could have worked in a professional circus but most of who were powerful, fairly wealthy, very successful businessmen.

A float carrying a band from Moose Jaw was scheduled to lead the parade. They had a decorated car that was supposed to pull the wagon bearing the men with their funny hats playing horns and drums. But the car that was pulling the float wouldn't start.

I asked some non-Shriners who were standing on the sidewalk, "What do you know about the Shriners?"

"They are silly," said one happy mother.

"They make me laugh," said another.

"They're old musicians and clowns," said a third.

It was painful to hear that so many knew so little about a group that has one goal, to help sick kids and charge them nothing. The Shriners operate some of the best hospitals in the world for children whose parents cannot afford medical care. Basically what they do is raise money and donate the money to this cause. When they are not raising money, they play. These are the kind of people I like.

They all come from the top ranks of the Freemasons, which is a secret society. My uncle was a Mason. When I lived with him, he would go into a closet to read his secret Masonic books, so the only thing I know about the Masons is that they are secret.

But when they reach the highest degree of seriousness and secretness, some of them become Shriners. Then they are anything but secret and everything they do seems to be the opposite of serious. Some are clowns, some musicians, some Keystone Kops. All of them are silly, mostly to make kids laugh. The only thing they keep secret is how much money they give to the hospitals. It is a large amount.

The motor of the car from Moose Jaw still would not start. So the band, cramped onto uncomfortable, fold-up metal chairs on the float that was going nowhere, began to play. They played while the band on the float from Salt Lake City took up the lead and passed them by. They played while the float from Sudbury passed them by.

They played while a mechanic from a gasoline alley fix-it shop under the Granville Bridge came out to listen to them.

"Do you know anything about the Shriners?" Jamie Forsythe asked him. Jamie is an editor who that day was operating the microwave truck for a live broadcast by the weather person, who was going to stand on the street in front of the parade so that there would be an interesting background while he gave the forecast.

To broadcast from downtown Vancouver means that the microwave antenna must be pointed toward a relay station on Mount Seymour. With all the new buildings going up along Pacific Boulevard it is impossible to see Mount Seymour, so Jamie and the other microwave operators have figured out ways to bounce the signal off one building, which sends it to another building, where it bounces again and possibly a third time before it ricochets up to the mountain. It is like playing billiards with microwaves. If you live in one of those buildings, you should have no fear. The microwave in your kitchen is bouncing many more of those same signals around the coffee you are heating up.

Back to the story: the mechanic was from India. He asked, "Shiners— are they car polishers?"

"No, Shriners are these guys who are stuck," said Jamie.

The mechanic still had no idea what Jamie was talking about, but he understood the word "stuck."

He opened the hood and a Shriner turned the key and the mechanic said it was probably the starter switch, and possibly the battery, which was being drained by someone trying to start an old car with a broken starter switch.

The mechanic tinkered while a band from Los Angeles passed the stalled float from Moose Jaw. He got out some tools and a battery charger and went back under the hood. A band from Seattle passed the band from Moose Jaw, and then a band from Calgary.

The last of the bands passed while the mechanic kept working. The parade was ending. The men in the funny hats from Moose Jaw climbed off the float that was going nowhere. They had come a long way to a great convention to be part of a wonderful parade, except they were stuck under a bridge with a dead engine.

So they did what Shriners do: they looked on the bright side. They surrounded the mechanic and began to play just for him. They played the "St. Louis Blues" because everyone loves that. And suddenly the mechanic walked around to the ignition key and turned it and the engine started.

The men clapped and climbed back onto the float. Most Shriners are in their sixties, some their seventies. Many of them don't pay as much attention to exercise as they do to charity, so the climb back up was not that quick.

By the time they were out on Pacific Boulevard the parade was basically over. They were two blocks behind the last float and the crowd was leaving. But you can't defeat a Shriner, especially one from Moose Jaw. Some of them stood up, and all of them raised their horns to the sky and blasted out the "St. Louis Blues" again in a way it had possibly never been heard, even in St. Louis.

The lone float at the end became a parade of its own, and the people along the route who had started leaving turned and came back. This was not just men in funny hats playing a song. This music sounded different. This had something in it that the folks at the curb could hear and that made them clap and cheer as the float went by.

The mechanic who had fixed the engine watched them as they faded away.

"Shriners," he said, "are good guys."

Abe's Junk Shop

I wish Abe had been my grandfather. I saw him one warm day leaning against the door jamb of his shop at Main and 28th. Over his head was a sign that said "Abe's Junk Shop."

How can you resist a junk shop?

"You vant junk?" he asked. He had an accent that was so musical I thought I was back in the deli where I used to buy my salami sandwiches when I was a kid. "I got junk."

Inside smelled of dust and treasures. There were hats, jewellery and suitcases and a spittoon and coats and shoes, and that was only in the corner to the left. To the right, watches and framed pictures of seashores and more coats were piled next to chairs and a set of bowling pins.

"You vant it, ve got it," he said. He had a smile. You could not picture Abe without a smile.

Abe was Polish and came to Vancouver shortly after the war. He had been a teenager in a concentration camp. Millions died, a figure that we throw out so easily, a statistic learned in school, but millions, unbelievable millions died, killed slowly through starvation and work that was torture, work that ended only when a human being ceased to be human any more, ceased to have the strength to keep breathing and fell and died. Millions died. Tens of thousands lived, including Abe.

He came as a refugee, and he made a cart out of wood and bicycle wheels and pulled it all over town looking for junk. He took the junk back to Main Street and stood on a corner and sold it. In time, he had enough money to rent a store. He put up a sign and got a truck and picked up more junk and sold it and married Goldie and had a son and worked hard for the next thirty years. He never slept in a doorway, he never asked for a dime. He never held out a paper cup for money. He never stood on a street corner asking for something with nothing to give in return.

I met Abe near the end of his working life. We did a story on his junk shop, and then we did a story on Morris, whose store was one away from Abe's, right on the corner of Main and 28th. Morris had the same background as Abe, but Morris was a little crazy.

Morris collected junk, but he would not sell it. If you picked up an old toaster off his shelf and asked, "How much?" Morris would take it from you and put it back.

"It's not for sale."

Then you would pick up a lamp.

"That's not for sale either."

"What about that coat?"

He would shake his head.

Morris loved his things. He had had nothing when he came here, and now he would not part with anything. On the sidewalk were sinks and toilets that he could not fit behind his door. He filled his shop with so much junk that there was no room to move. You could open the front door and step in, but you could go no farther.

The fire department closed Morris down because his shop was a fire trap. He got a storeroom somewhere and moved some of his stuff into it and reopened. But he still would not sell anything. I have no idea how he lived, but he did fine. No welfare, no handouts. Somewhere along the line he sold enough to keep going.

Then he died.

Abe grew old and passed his shop on to his son, who changed the name to "Abe's Furniture." He got rid of the junk and stocked antique furnishings.

I saw Abe a few years later standing in the doorway. His son had taken a vacation. Abe never took a vacation.

"I don't understand him," said Abe. "Junk is good. Does he think he is too good for junk? I don't understand kids."

Main and 28th is now the centre for endless antique shops and coffee shops and boutiques and bakeries. No junk shops. No Abe. No Morris. No one saying, "You vant it, I got it." It is becoming a trendy place to live and shop. Despite that, I would still like to live there.

But I think if Abe or Morris came back they would seize an opportunity. They would get a pushcart and say, "It's not a real neighbourhood unless it has a good junk shop. You never know when you will need something only we have."

Submarine Guy

"**D**ive, dive."

Captain Hutchinson pulled the handle on a lever marking the depth at twenty metres, his periscope level.

"We are slipping below the Pacific," he said.

Soon we were down in the silence, cruising so smoothly it was hard to believe we were moving unseen at eight knots, heading possibly toward battle, but more than likely toward just another training mission.

The captain checked the sonar, then slid out of his command chair. We could see each other, he and I, but barely. There were so many pipes, tubes and gauges that we had to crane our necks to get a view of each other's faces, and we were only two arms' lengths apart. The innards of a battle-ready ship leave little room for comfort.

Along the sides of the hull were banks of radios, sonar equipment, decoders, encoders, dials, switches and steel grey boxes whose use only a submariner would know.

"Levelling off now," he said into a small microphone to someone, somewhere. "Now, what would you like to know?" he said to me.

"Why?" I said, that being the basis of all my questions.

"Why?" replied the fiftyish captain, who had been in charge of this vessel for almost ten years. "Because it is a beautiful way to live, to sail, to see the world and not be seen."

He checked his readings, reset some gauges, then looked up with a serious face. "Just routine patrol today."

Now let's jump back a week earlier. I was in the library in New Westminster when a woman said to me, "You've got to see this. You won't believe it."

"What?"

"You'll think I'm crazy, but there's a submarine on someone's balcony."

I was thinking: She is not crazy, but she wants to show me a model of a submarine, possibly an extremely large model, filling an entire balcony, maybe even extending over the sides of the balcony. I was thinking: I do not want to go to see such a model. I have done stories on models before, and they are not always exciting.

"Please," she said, "you've got to see it."

I followed her out the door, and we began walking down Ash Street, which is just behind the library. It was dark, and I was thinking: This woman must really want me to see that submarine. It is raining and dark, and she is going out of her way. I will show her the respect of going along.

But before I could think anything else she said, "There. Look."

She pointed up, and I was looking at the second-floor balcony of an apartment house at Ash and 5th streets. On the balcony was clearly half the firepower of the entire Canadian Navy. There was a cannon, a radar dish, cowling, pipes, supports, rigging and other things, many other things, all navy-issue grey and packed onto the balcony with the expertise only a military loadmaster could possess.

And then Captain Bruce Hutchinson's head surfaced over the firepower. He waved.

The lovely lady left, and I never saw her again. But I often thank her.

I knocked on the door to the captain's apartment.

"Welcome aboard," he said.

"Is this legal?" I asked in innocence. What else could you say to someone who is so far outside the mainstream that he must be breaking uncountable rules and regulations?

"Perfectly and totally," he said.

Everything Captain Hutchinson owns is navy surplus, sold on the open market. Everything was paid for with honest Canadian cash. The captain has no car, and he could not get most of the stuff on a bus, so he carried it on foot from a military surplus store on the other side of New Westminster.

The only battle he has fought is with City Hall, which told him he must surely be violating some rules and regulations. After all, you can't have a submarine inside your apartment that spills out onto the balcony. What will people say?

But Captain Hutchinson raised the victory flag. There were no rules and no regulations to say you could not have a submarine of your very own. No building codes were being violated; there were no complaints from neighbours. In fact, the captain is an institution in the neighbourhood. The residents he is keeping safe from enemy attack are annoyed only by the people who stop on the sidewalk and say, "What the heck is that?"

Bruce Hutchinson has no room to cook in the kitchen of his apartment, which has been converted into a command centre. He eats most of his meals in the food court of the New West mall, which is a block away. He has no room to sleep in his bedroom, which has been converted into the crew's quarters. The bunks are packed in so tightly no human sailor could actually get into them, so he sleeps on the floor, just inside his apartment door, the only place in his home where you can take three steps in a row. When he isn't eating or sleeping, he spends his time silently patrolling just below the water-line to keep this country safe.

Crazy?

No more than William Randolph Hearst, who built a castle in California. Chances are you when you visit the castle, you will say, "What imagination!"

And no more crazy than former premier Bill Vander Zalm, who built Fantasy Gardens, which included a castle that was a miniature replica of one from the town in Holland Captain George Vancouver's family came from.

And no more crazy than you, when you built a backyard fort or tree-house as a kid and said you never wanted to grow up and leave it.

Captain Bruce Hutchinson has not lost that sense of wonder and make-believe. As you read this, he is running silent and deep and is the captain of his own ship. That's more than most of us can say.

Message in a Bottle

It was raining. No, it was pouring. The cameraman and I were unloading his equipment from the van and wondering what we were doing at our advanced ages working on a Sunday morning in the rain because someone had found a note in an old house.

Worse yet, the cameraman, Dave McKay, had to go to the bathroom, and you can't walk into someone's house and say, "Hello, pleased to meet you, and may I, someone you don't know, use your bathroom and after that we will act professional?"

So he drove off looking for a toilet. All the exciting stuff about news is true. But the human condition is also true, and that can influence life as well as news. After Dave was gone I was left alone in the rain on a Sunday morning wondering what I was doing getting wet on a street I had never been on because someone had found a note in an old house.

There was no bell at the front door of the house. I knocked, and there was no answer. Probably I had the wrong day, or the wrong house. Dave McKay would not be pleased. I was not pleased. I was wet. But just then a young guy came around from the back of the house carrying a hammer and some boards.

"Why are you standing in the rain?" asked the young guy, whose name was Victor.

I followed him around back and saw what everyone who has ever renovated a house will recognize: disaster. Outside were piles of wood and panelling that had been inside. Inside were walls that were exposed and more loose panelling and air full of dust and more work than any human being should ever have to face.

"Here it is." He showed me a parcel wrapped in aluminum foil. "I found it behind the cabinet, right up here."

"Don't tell me yet," I said.

Stories are never told well twice. The first time they are filled with energy and raw truth: "I found it behind the cabinet. I couldn't believe it." But by the time the camera is there, the same line becomes: "I was working far later than my wife wanted me to because she was having relatives for dinner and she wanted me home, and I thought I would get this cabinet down but I wondered if she would be mad at me so I pulled quickly, but it was stuck over there, in that corner, you see, right where your head is, and I pulled and it didn't come down at first and . . ."

So I hate stories told twice, and I was hoping Dave would come back soon.

Victor, however, was undaunted. He started to open the package.

"Don't. Wait," I said.

But by then it was open and he handed it to me. I saw a newspaper from 1962 and a headline that read, "Russians Test New A-Bomb."

"And here's the note that came with it."

It was from someone named Gladys Haughton, who wrote, "I don't know if the world will be here long after I am gone. Everything has gone crazy. Everyone is getting ready for war."

I remembered 1962 and the Cuban Missile Crisis. I remembered standing in front of a ten-inch black-and-white TV in our apartment watching President Kennedy facing down the Russians. I remember knowing that the world could come to an end in the next few hours, and that is no exaggeration.

I went to the other end of our apartment to tell my mother what was happening. She was sitting at the tiny kitchen table staring at a cup of tea.

"I don't want to hear about it," she said.

My mother was born during World War I. She had a baby, me, during World War II. She left her husband during the Korean War. Her son would be drafted during the Vietnam War. She lived with reports about atomic bombs during most of her adult life, especially when she became a grandmother. And she did not know it then, but she would die during the first Gulf War. And she would have become a grandmother during the Iraq War.

She had a right not to want to hear about it.

But Victor was determined to tell me his story and he would not stop.

"Look, she's talking about the world ending. That could not have happened, could it?"

Victor Maratumo is Japanese Canadian. Gladys Haughton's note said she had moved into the house in 1940, and shortly after that, Victor's forefathers and mothers in this fine land were rounded up and put into camps. Everything they owned was taken from them: their homes, their fishing boats, their schools, their lives. They were locked up, even those who had been born in Canada and were citizens.

What could not have happened did happen.

And the old reporter, who was now looking at the note left by a sweet woman, remembered being taught to duck and cover before Victor was born. Almost every day in P.S. 54, the teacher would shout, "Duck and cover." At those words, kids across the United States and Canada would automatically fall off their chairs and squeeze themselves under their desks and cover the backs of their necks with their hands waiting for the blinding flash and the giant blast that would blow in the windows and spray broken glass all over us.

That would be the first wave of the attack. And we all knew that at the moment the windows were blown in, missiles from America would be blasting off to destroy Russia, and the waves of B-52 bombers that were constantly in the air would not be called back.

That giant tsunami of bombers took off every four hours from bases all across the northern US. They flew toward the Soviet Union with orders to keep going and destroy their targets unless called back before the fail-safe line.

Six flights a day, hundreds of planes in each flight, around the clock, from 1949 to 1990 headed north without missing a beat. The pilots were flying toward death. On the other side of the world, the same armada with different markings on their planes was coming our way.

My cousin, Dick Reichert, who slept in the hallway after my mother and I moved into his family's apartment, was a flight-line mechanic at an air base in Montana. He fixed the bombers that headed north. He expected that one day they would not return. Four years after the Cuban Missile Crisis I was stationed at an air base in Florida with planes on every runway aimed at Cuba. I understood what Gladys had been worried about.

Before long, Dave came back with his camera, looking relieved. Victor was so excited that he went through his story again like it was the first time, disproving everything I thought about people not being able to tell the same story twice. I guess a good story never gets tired.

Also in Gladys's note was the worry that her husband would not get the kitchen cabinets up straight. Wives worry about things like nuclear destruction and cabinets. She worried too that her beloved home would be knocked down someday. She had such a good life here, she wrote. It was her first and last house, bought in 1940, and she lived in it until she died in 2004.

"It will be a lot of work to renovate this house," said Victor, "but I liked it even before I found the note."

The letter is now hung on a rebuilt wall inside the suddenly young-again house. Wherever she is, Gladys must feel better that the letter, her house and the world are still here. And the kitchen cabinets are hung perfectly straight.

And the bathroom works fine. I asked.

Jerry of Cassiar

He is the king of the hill. He is the white-haired, white-bearded official greeter for cars going north and south over the Ironworkers Memorial bridge. He is the smile of the day and the cleaning machine and the road repair crew and the guy who has inspired more phone calls to me than anyone else in the last ten years.

"Hey, have you seen the guy at Hastings and Cassiar? I mean, I can't describe him but he's amazing."

"Yo. You want a good story, go to Hastings and Cassiar. There's this guy there who, well, you got to see him for yourself."

"Listen, Ducky. I called you last week about the guy at Hastings and Cassiar and you didn't do anything about him. If you ignore him, I'm never going to watch you again."

She didn't leave her phone number. She hadn't left it the week before when I wanted to call her back and say, "Madam. If you had been paying attention you would have seen two stories on him. But no. You don't leave your number and now you think I am a schmuck and how can I tell you that I know Jerry of Cassiar is the king of the hill?"

I watched him for weeks, then months at, well, you know where. He just waves. He doesn't ask for money or handouts. He waves. And he picks up garbage. He picks up cigarette butts and stray pieces of paper. In fact, the northbound entrance onto the highway off Hastings and Cassiar is the cleanest corner in the city. All thanks to Jerry.

So I said to myself, one day I'll do a story about him, he is always there. He's like an ace up my sleeve, something for sure in my back pocket. And then that day came. I could find nothing else, and I said to the cameraman, let's go to Hastings and Cassiar because there is this guy with white hair and a white beard who is always there and he waves to cars and there is probably something amazing about him.

The cameraman said he hoped so because it was late in the day and we were running out of light as well as time to shoot it.

No sweat, I said. He's always there.

We arrived at Hastings and Cassiar. No one was there.

But, I said. But. But something is wrong.

We drove into the PNE in the desperate hope of finding something, anything. Sometimes things have been good on the PNE grounds, like the time in the off-season when we saw the animals from the petting zoo grazing below the roller coaster. It turned out that they wintered in the grass under the ride. More importantly, they were watched over by a shepherd, an actual, official, licenced shepherd.

"You're not a real shepherd, are you?" I asked the shepherd.

"Yep," he said. "Real as they come. Just like in the Bible."

He had taken a course offered by some college in BC and got his shepherding licence and there he was. In the summer he was a mechanic on the rides, but in the winter he wandered among the forest of four by fours that support the roller coaster and tended his flock of goats and geese and lambs. That was a touching story.

But the shepherd was not there this time when I needed him. And the couple who were grooms at the track but could not live in the barns because they had a dog and dogs are not allowed at the track so they pitched a tent at the edge of the parking lot and lived in it: they were not there either.

Could life be any more cruel? It was nearly 4:00 p.m. and I had nothing. I would be fired. Worse than that, I would quit because I could no longer do this job. How could I be expected to find a story every day? That was impossible. That took more kindness from the story god than anyone deserves.

"Take me back to my car," I said to the cameraman. Those were the words of defeat.

We drove out of the parking lot and up to Cassiar and there, in front of us, was a white-haired man with a white beard waving to passing cars.

"See, he's always there."

We parked and ran across the street. I asked if we could take his picture, and he said, "It's about time. So many people tell me they are calling you about me and you never show up."

You know, some days you just let your shoulders and your head drop, and you admit defeat even in the face of victory. How could I say, "I was saving you for a rainy day and this is that day, but you have already caused me to have one heart attack. Don't, please, don't take revenge and say no, and by the way, where were you?"

"I had to go to the bathroom," he said.

He had used the toilet in the McDonald's across the street and got back just a minute ago. If we had left the PNE parking lot two minutes sooner, we would have missed him.

As it turned out, my first story on Jerry of Cassiar was about a spirited guy who was homeless and living in the Catholic Charities Men's Hostel and spent his days waving to cars.

"I never ask for money. I never ask for anything. I just say hello and how you doing?"

It is true. Jerry says, "Hello, how you doing? You're looking good, young fellow." Then he waves and the light changes and the cars go. He asks for nothing and gives a compliment in return.

He does not carry a sign that says, "Help me. Life is unfair. Spare change. God bless you."

In return he gets coins and sandwiches and apples and smiles and waves and friends who call a TV station and say he should be on the air. He also picks up litter. Between lights he scours the gutters alongside the curbs and removes everything that gets dropped there. By the end of a day, he has filled several plastic buckets with litter. Can you imagine how that corner would look without him? No, don't imagine it. Go to most other intersections and look at the oceans of garbage that just lie there and collect more oceans of garbage.

But on this day Jerry did more than pick up litter and say hello. He saved my job. Thanks, Jerry.

Two weeks later, I drove by Jerry's corner.

"Hey, where's my copy of the story?" he said.

"Whoops," I said, "sorry, I didn't remember, where are you going to play it, I thought you were homeless, I'll get it for you tomorrow."

You've got to talk fast before the light changes.

"I want to send it to my son in Alberta."

Darn, how could I have forgotten? He let us film him. He talked to me. He asked for one thing, a copy of what we said about him, and I forgot, because I am a busy guy, running around like a mindless bobblehead trying to keep my job.

Two lessons. I bet if Jimmy Pattison had asked for a copy of a story, I would have had it delivered by courier a few hours later. Lesson number one: Move all Jerrys up to the Jimmy category. And I bet if I hadn't been so excited about impressing a producer by sneaking in under the wire once again, I would have had room in my head to think about someone else. Lesson number two: When you're picking up your advanced university diploma, remember it was your mother who taught you to print your name.

The next day I handed Jerry a tape.

This does not happen often, but after that came two more stories on Jerry. One we shot later that year, at Christmas, when he decorated his corner with a small branch and some ribbons. The next story was about the sign at Cassiar and Hastings.

"See the sign?" said Jerry through the car window. "I put it up myself."

"What sign?"

"That sign."

And then the light changed.

I parked the car and walked back to him. The sign at the corner that warns traffic to avoid a six-inch-high concrete road-divider was gone. The sign had been knocked down, probably by a drunk driver who was seeing cross-eyed and ran straight into it.

The day he noticed the sign was down, Jerry told a passing police car. Next he told a passing city works truck. Then he took one of his quarters and called City Hall. Later in the day he called again. The next morning he called. And at lunchtime, and in the afternoon. The following day he called City Hall again. The missing sign was costing him all his quarters.

Jerry showed me the hubcaps that had been knocked off the cars that had hit the road divider because there was now no sign warning them about it.

Bang.

"What the heck was that?"

"A concrete road-divider, I think."

"#!@!#! Why don't they put up a sign warning people about it?"

Jerry showed me more than thirty hubcaps.

"Expensive repairs," said Jerry, "and some of these cars could have flipped over."

He was right. A front wheel hitting a six-inch concrete abutment dead-on could throw a car on its side.

Jerry found part of a wooden barricade and a plastic orange cone near Homer Street, where he started his morning. He put the piece of wood over his shoulder and picked up the cone and got on a bus and carried them to Hastings and Cassiar. There he made his own road-dividing sign, using some glow-in-the-dark orange tape he had found somewhere else and a piece of cardboard on which he drew arrows indicating "don't go here."

He was super proud of his sign. It was there for three days before I was able to get back to him, and during that time not one hubcap got knocked off. Not one driver got shocked out of his wits and said really bad words. Jerry was a one-man street crew who cost no taxpayer dollars and did not need a series of forms and requisitions authorizing him to begin the job.

I did a story on Jerry and his sign. The next morning, before Jerry got to his corner, a city street crew put up a real sign and took away Jerry's wood and tape.

Jerry spent the day getting thumbs-up and cheers from passing drivers, thanking a homeless guy for keeping the city repaired.

There's Seaweed in Here

It was a beautiful day. The sun filled the sky, and Eric Cable, the Rocky Mountain of a legend of a cameraman, who has a wish of exposing all the bad people in the world, and I were heading up the coast to do a story about the herring roe fishery.

Roe is a fancy word for fish eggs. Caviar is a fancy word for roe, which is something you put on cream cheese to stop the roe from sliding off the cracker onto the floor and ruining your night when you spill your wine while trying to pick it up. Roe can cost you a lot of wine. Some of your guests will love it, and some will say, "Fish eggs? Yuck."

Okay, I admit I like it. But there's no excuse for killing a whole fish just to get a taste of its unborn children. If we did that to chickens, we would have no chickens.

Most of the roe used to go to Japan, where they make an art out of eating things that the rest of us thought were uneatable twenty years ago. But styles change, and now we line up for raw fish and rice covered with fish eggs. So the demand for roe is up, even though the number of fish dying to give it to us is down.

Eric and I were hoping to film an official fisheries department opening because herring fishing is a zoo, a rodeo, a gladiator sport on the water. The winner makes a year's salary in half an hour and the losers are too embarrassed to sail home. The boats circle round and round waiting for an air horn to sound. The horn blower in turn is waiting for a fish biologist's signal that enough of the swollen mommy herrings have made it to shore, where they will lay their eggs while the males wriggle and shoot sperm over them.

Herring have sex once in their lifetime, which is about what some older married men feel they are accomplishing.

The air horn blows loudly enough to break your eardrum, and the boats take off like racers on a drag strip. There are virtually no rules. Some ships team up with helicopters that circle overhead looking for the herring, which swarm in balls as big as half a basketball court. Some captains use sonar fish finders, some rely on hunches and the look of the ripples on the water. The pilots are tough and mean and hungry and unforgiving and skilled and ferocious. It is wise not to get in their way. They make circles inside other circles and if someone cuts through their circles they go around again and take revenge with a tighter circle. The boats outmanoeuvre each other, cut each other off and just plain cheat. There is no love lost at a herring opening.

Eric and I had come up by float plane and boat to a location near Bella Coola. Besides being a cameraman, Eric is an artist, the kind who works with oil paints and brushes and canvas. He is very good, but like most undiscovered artists he sells some of his paintings while keeping many in his garage. Someday, after he is long dead, his paintings will probably be worth a fortune, but meanwhile he is a television cameraman with worn-out joints from playing too much rugby. On this sunny day, while we waited for the fishery to open, he began taking video pictures of shorelines and fish boats, which I knew he would later paint.

"What are you shooting?" I asked. I have been with cameramen who have run out of tape, and I did not want Eric to waste tape on anything that was not related to the story.

"I'm just doing scenery," said Eric.

I was wishing that he would not waste tape, but I could not say this because he is as old as me, and has as much experience. He and I have spent months together in northern British Columbia and the Yukon, sleeping in the back of vans and in construction trailers and drinking out of the same beer can. I should not be telling him what to do.

"Don't look so worried," he said. "I'm putting in a fresh tape for you."

"I wasn't worried," I said.

"I know that," he said. "It's just your face that was panicking."

Eric changed the tapes just as the horn blew. Experienced cameramen have a talent for knowing when to be ready.

The boats started fighting each other for position. I could not believe how vicious and nasty the captains were until I remembered that the ones who filled their nets would be rich for a year and those who did not would be bitter for the same length of time.

Eric filmed without taking his finger off the button. There were waves and curses and crashes and nets almost bursting with crushes of silver payloads.

It was over in ten minutes. Ten minutes of hauling in tons of wriggling, horny males and pregnant females, and Eric had shot it like a champion. He had everything. He had crashing boats and cursing captains and bursting fishnets. I was as happy as I could get this side of warm bodily contact.

Our boat took us back to the dock where the float plane had dropped us off. When we'd arrived that morning, the sea was calm and the step up from the pontoon to the dock was easy. Now the wind had kicked up, and the plane was floating one large step out. The pilot held out his hand for me. I took it and made the half-jump to the pontoon.

Then I turned around.

"Let me have the tapes," I said.

I held out my hand, but I could not reach the tape in Eric's outstretched hand.

"Toss it to me," I said.

"Are you crazy?" he asked.

"I can catch," I said indignantly. I grew up playing baseball. I could catch something being thrown two feet.

"Are you sure?"

"Sure!"

He tossed the tape and I caught it. Are you kidding? It was no contest. I played second base on the street when I was ten.

He threw the second tape just as a small wave went under the pontoon. And right where my practiced catching hand was stretched out waiting for the tape, suddenly there was nothing but air. Every bit of my baseball instinct shot my hand down and my fingers managed to bang into the plastic case and knock it into the vast Pacific Ocean.

I remember watching the tape start to sink. I remember it in slow motion. I remember seeing it go down and down. I remember saying to myself, you idiot; you are in deep trouble. Then I remember the pilot dropping to his knee and plunging his arm into the water up to his shoulder and grabbing the box in mid-descent to the bottom of the ocean. My God, he must be a good pilot. His reaction was quicker than my fear of how I was going to be fired.

"Here," he said, handing it to me with water pouring out of the box.

"You idiot," shouted Eric. "You flipping, brainless idiot who can't catch."

We flew back to Vancouver holding the tape next to a heater under the seats.

I had no idea which tape it was, the pretty pictures or the battling boats.

Back in the office, the editor put the tape we'd dried into one of the playback decks, a big machine filling up a corner of the room.

He pushed a button and something flashed across the screen. Ocean. Thank goodness. The tape was working.

After a second, though, the ocean froze in mid-wave and dissolved into static on the screen. Static is not good.

"Bad?" I asked the editor.

"Does it look good?"

Then the machine stopped.

The editor called an engineer. Engineers in newsrooms are like medics on a battlefield. The come bearing screwdrivers and flashlights. They love touching injured machines and bringing them back to life.

"What's wrong?"

"It's broken."

Engineers always prefer technical explanations.

He opened the top of the deck, peered down into the darkness with his flashlight, reached in with a set of needle-nosed pliers and lifted something out.

"There's seaweed in here," he said. "This is not in the manual. I don't know how to deal with seaweed."

He took the tape out and cleaned the machine. The editor tried the other tape. We could see right away it had pictures of boats. Sometimes you get lucky. Half an hour later the story was on the air.

Eric, like all artists, went back to the drawing board. "You probably ruined a masterpiece," he said.

"I'll keep painting," he told me. "You keep trying to learn to catch."

The Banker and the Horses

I t is easy to have a dream. You simply say this is what I want to do, and then
you listen to your friends say, "You're a nut case. You're insane. That's a
stupid dream. You will regret it for the rest of your life."

Ed Thompson was a young banker on his way up. He worked for the
Bank of Montreal. He wore a suit. He was not happy.

Ed wanted to train horses.

"Train horses, are you crazy?"

That's what his fellow young bankers on the way up said.

"Train horses to do what? Count?"

They shook their corporate heads.

"Train racehorses," Ed said.

Okay, that was more than insane. Training horses was one thing, but
racehorses? The racetrack is no place for a banker.

But Ed loved horses. All his life he had watched and admired horses, and
he couldn't take his eyes off them. He thought the horse was one of the most
magnificent animals on God's earth, something built for power and speed, a
creature that looked like it took an unspeakable joy in running. When horses
run in a pack, you can see the pride in each horse trying to be the fastest, trying to be in front.

And so was born the first racetrack.

They gave Ed a farewell party at the bank, but he was the only one smiling. With no job, no prospects, no experience, he went to the track at the PNE and looked for work. He found it as a groom, putting in nearly twenty hours a day during the race season. Like many grooms, whose pay would not fill up a corner of a bank teller's petty cash drawer, he slept in the barns at the track.

If the fellows back at the bank had seen Ed, they would have smirked. They were right. There was Ed shovelling manure, hauling water and oats, walking sweating horses and brushing them and putting saddles on them for others to ride and get the glory. Ed worked from before sunrise till after sunset. But he stuck with it, watching the horses and watching how the trainers watched the horses. They studied the muscles and the gait and how a horse held its head. They devised individual programs for each horse: gallop, then race, then gallop, then rest, to make the horse's legs and lungs strong and to get the most out of their running.

After several years of working hard and looking like he knew what he was doing, someone trusted Ed to train a horse. He did, and it won, and nothing is more valued at the racetrack than winning. Ed soon had a few more horses to train, and they won too. Then more horses, with the same result.

By the time I met Ed, he was on the list of the ten most winning trainers at the track. His training barn was just a few steps from the paddock, meaning it was in a number-one position. He was making a lot more money than a bank executive did.

I was thrilled to do a story about Ed, though he did not say more than ten words that day. In the twenty years I've known him since, he has spoken fewer than fifteen words on each meeting.

"I'm fine. How are you? I have this new horse that looks good."

One day, walking along West Hastings Street not far from the SeaBus, Ed saw someone, and for a moment his legs refused to move.

"Is it you?" he asked the woman.

She looked at him and smiled.

"Of course it's me," she said, knowing who she was and knowing who he was. "And I know it's you. But it's strange to see you without a suit."

It was more than twenty years since they had seen each other. Gillian

Campbell was the first and only woman Ed had ever loved. Face to face on a busy street, with people rushing around them, they looked into each other's eyes.

So many stories, so much to say, so they said nothing. They just looked at each other. Ed and Gillian had been in love. Then something had happened, as it often does. She had married someone else and had two sons and then divorced. She went on to a singing career in the Yukon, performing as Klondike Kate, and Ed went on to the bank. Decades passed before this moment when eternity was just beginning.

At Ed and Gillian's wedding, half the guests were roughnecks from the track and half were entertainers. Six-foot-six showgirls danced with four-foot-two jockeys. The newly married couple rode off in a horse-drawn carriage and have been happy ever since. He goes to her concerts and she shovels his manure.

One afternoon at the track, while I was at the rail shouting the magical, "Come on, seven, come on, seven," like the horse knew his number was seven and could hear me, I spotted some businessmen in suits who had come to the track for an outing. They were bonding, that was clear. They had beer, and they had scratch sheets that none of them could read.

I slid over close to listen.

"Wouldn't it be great to work down here?" one of them said. "You'd have freedom. You'd live by your wits."

Another one watched the horses crossing the finish line. He buttoned his thousand-dollar suit jacket. "Don't even think of it," he said. "This place is full of people who couldn't make it in the real world."

I could see Ed down at the paddock getting ready for the next race. He was wearing a beat-up sweater and a worn-out cowboy hat and was giving last-minute instructions to a jockey.

Would I put my money on the suits or the sweater?

You don't have to ask.

PNE Fishpond

Yes, I know it seemed cruel. But it was freedom and excitement like those fish had never known, even if it only lasted a few days. If you are going to be born a goldfish in a pet store, there are usually only two alternatives. One is getting scooped out of your tank and put into another tank with much larger, very hungry fish and swimming for your life until the teeth sink into your body. It is not fun to be a feeder fish. The last thing you see is the inside of the throat of another fish.

Or you can be bought by someone who wants a cheap pet. In that case, you wind up in a bowl that is the equivalent of a solitary confinement cell and spend your life swimming one stroke here, till you come to a glass wall, then one stroke there, till you come to a glass wall. Since the oxygen is low and the food too plentiful, you die stuffed and sluggish in a week or two.

So what the PNE guy did was not so bad.

It was raining a lot during the PNE that year, sometime in the early nineties. There were many stories about attendance being down and fairgoers getting soggy. But I was having a ball.

The PNE was the first country fair I had ever seen. In 1973, my first time there, it was much larger than it is now, and there were jam competitions and pie contests and that wonderful giant map of BC in the sports hall of fame. The map was so big you rode over it on a movable bridge and looked down at the cities and towns and mountains and rivers of the province. It was made of pieces of plywood, some of which were piled up into the shapes of mountains and valleys, and the rivers were long, coloured wires. It was crude, rough and incredible. Ask anyone who went to the fair back then to describe this land of British Columbia and they can. Ask someone now to describe it.

There were also the cows and pigs and chickens and horses. Back then each breed had its own barn. Now there is just a small sampling of animals all living together under one roof.

But now and then don't matter. I fell in love with the fair, and in the thirty years since, I have been lucky enough to go to the PNE every year on almost every working day and do a new story. Many of these have been on the hucksters who sell Ginsu knives and potato peelers and chamois cloths. They are magicians in the art of psychology. In just thirty seconds they can tell you about their product, show you the incredibly unbelievable things their product can do, like remove dirt from something that is dirty or cut through a tomato using only a sharp blade, and create in you the desire to own their product above all other products in the world. If only you had that thing, that new improved thing, life would be so much better. Then you buy it, and you can't wait to get home to clean the silverware. Wait a minute. You don't have any silverware.

One time cameraman Eric Cable and I were talking to a man selling kitchen knives.

"I can sell anything," the man said.

"Anything?" asked Eric. Eric knew he had something that was truly useless. This was back in the days of film cameras, and each roll of film was wound around a small inner core of yellow plastic. The cores looked like a wheel about the size of your thumb and index finger placed together in a circle and were hollow on the inside. They were thrown out after use. If you dig through old landfills, you can still find them.

"How about this?" said Eric, handing the man a useless yellow film core.

Eric's camera was rolling. He was hoping, like me, that the wizard salesman would say something like, "I mean, I can sell anything that has some value or some use, not something like this."

Whoops. Don't ever underestimate a carnival huckster. They survive by getting money out of your pocket. How they do it is sheer genius.

Without missing a beat, without blinking, without thinking and worrying and calling his agent or pulling out a manual or asking for an extension, the man said: "The chance of a lifetime is waiting for you right here. For a dollar, one small dollar, get a lovely yellow bonsai planter, napkin holder, and massage wheel all in one."

He demonstrated how the film core could relieve the tension of a day when rolled across your back or arms or hand. "And for only one dollar, how can you go wrong?"

The man not only sold the film core, he put in an order to Eric for all the film cores he could come up with. Eric, who always tries to help his fellow human beings, pulled a sack of fifty out of his supply bag. Within five minutes the huckster had sold them all.

You can either go to university and get an MBA, or go to the PNE and watch and learn from someone selling a mop that actually, amazingly, will get your floor clean. He will soon have your money and you will have a mop.

"Don't you have a mop at home?"

"Not one that cleans like this. It cleans cleaner than clean, he said."

But I was talking about the fish. As I mentioned, it had rained a lot that year. Business was down, and one of the guys working at the giant containers just outside the gates of the fair was bored. His job was to keep kewpie dolls supplied to the carnival area, where you could win one by getting the ring over the Coke bottle, which you would spend ten dollars trying to do to get the twenty-five-cent doll.

But the rain was keeping the ring throwers away, and so the kewpie dolls were sleeping deep in the big containers. They were the kind of containers that come in on ships and are hauled away on trucks and then sit on the ground on stumps of legs just high enough to slip the prongs of a forklift under.

The containers were dripping with rain, which made puddles. The puddles were everywhere. Fairgoers and PNE employees jumped them, sloshed through them and, if they were really fussy, walked around them. One puddle poked out a few steps past the first container and stretched underneath it and the next four containers, which were all lined up in a row.

What a perfect place for some goldfish. The fellow came to work one day with a plastic bag holding a hundred tiny creatures that had been spared the choppers of bigger fish. He dumped them in, and the puddle suddenly became a frenzy of water and goldfish. The excited fish took off, some of them swimming in a straight line, something they had never done in their lives, going and going and going. The puddle was two or three inches deep in some places, so there was more than enough room for a fish to fly with a freedom that we can only imagine.

In goldfish terms, the puddle was endless. You could see them scooting between the containers and underneath them and eventually coming out the other side. Only then did they have to turn around and, in a thrilling marathon, begin to make their way back. There was so much to see on the trip, rocks and pebbles and weeds and other fish just like themselves, and no one was chasing them. The fellow also bought a big can of fish food, so at one end there was a banquet the fish could feast on before getting back into the race.

The freedom lasted more than a week. PNE officials were not happy about it. They didn't care about the fish, even after I did a story on them. All they were interested in were the weather reports, which continued to be goldfish—not people—friendly.

And then the sun came out and the fair got crowded and the puddles started to dry up, and one day I saw there was nothing left but a very small puddle hidden in the shade under one container. The man who had set the goldfish free was now busy supplying the ring-throwing booths with kewpie dolls. By the time the fair ended, the puddle was gone. I never saw any fish bodies. Probably a lucky animal got some sushi for dinner, so that everything was recycled.

But for one shining week, a school of tiny, innocently condemned creatures had a ball. To the guy whose name I lost with my notes ten years ago, you did good.

Those Little Donuts

There is one product at the PNE that sells better than anything else there. It outsells shredders that cut lettuce without shredding your fingers. It outsells mops that actually mop up spills. And it outsells the burgers covered with onions at Jimmy's Lunch, which has been selling burgers at the fair since 1939 and is very good at selling burgers.

If you have read the title above, you already remember how they taste and how warm they are and how the cinnamon and sugar on them are so good you eat five of them before you realize you haven't offered any to your patient father, even though he paid for them. You watch them come out of the machine while you wait in line. There is always a line because it is hard to go to the fair and not get a bag of those little donuts.

"Once we are inside can we get, what do you call them, those little donuts? I forget what you call them, but you know what I mean."

"Yup, I don't know what they're called either, but I know, it's those little donuts. I want some too."

And in a minute there is the sign that says "Those Little Donuts." You get in line and watch them being made, kerplunk, sizzle, kerplunk, sizzle. You are being hypnotized. You want those little donuts. You get a bag, and they are so warm you start eating, and then you eat some more, and now you can move on to the roller coaster.

"Oh my gosh, my stomach is not feeling good. Why did I eat those little donuts?"

Because you are weak. Because you are human. Because you have waited a year for them. And during the two weeks of the fair more than two million will be sold.

"We're not supposed to tell how many, but that's about right," said Steve Johnson, who owns Those Little Donuts.

"Is this all you do?" I ask him and his wife, Annette. "I mean, do you have another job? Usually people working at the fair have to have another job to keep going."

Well, they say, there are four other fairs they go to between here and Calgary.

"And how many days do you work all year?"

After some jesting, they admit it comes down to about three months of work a year. The rest of the time they spend on their tiny eight-acre hobby farm in Alberta and their slightly larger twenty-acre mini-ranch in Texas. All from those little donuts, an item that started life as a dismal, money-losing failure.

The story of those little donuts begins on Christmas Eve, 1958, with the opening of the Walt Disney movie *Tom Thumb*. It is based on an old fairy tale about two little people who are the size of an average-sized hand. They have to fight off an evil giant.

The picture won several Academy Awards. But Walt Disney made one of his few career mistakes in connection with that movie. He thought that people watching a movie about tiny people would like to nibble on tiny donuts. Wrong. No matter what is on the screen, whether it is chainsaw massacres or penguins in the Antarctic or thumb-sized heroes, those in their seats eat popcorn—sometimes chocolate, sometimes gummy drops, but 99 per cent of the time it is popcorn. It is never donuts.

That Walt Disney, who created Mickey Mouse as well as Disneyland, did not know this proves that no one knows everything, even though Walt came close. The movie did well—the donuts did not, so Walt ordered the destruction of all one thousand of his Tom Thumb donut machines.

Somehow six of them got left in a warehouse, and a few years later a man hunting for a bargain bought them during a cleaning-out sale held by the movie company. The bargain hunter was Steve Johnson's father. He gave the machines to his son and said, see what you can do with these.

Since then, Steve has had made many more donut machines, all based on the original design. A movie theatre is not a good place for a little donut, but a fairground is the perfect home.

It's like the chemist who was trying to invent a substitute for rubber during World War II. He invented something that was gummy and bounced. It never became rubber; instead it became Silly Putty, one of the greatest toys of all time.

And there was the English scientist eighty years ago who was upset because one of his Petri dishes was contaminated with a mould. Presto: penicillin.

But why the name, "Those Little Donuts"? Why not a real name? I asked.

"We couldn't think of anything else," said Steve.

He Had a Big One

I try to avoid sex. I mean, I have standards, and sex is for those who try to boost ratings and leave everyone happy. Who wants that? I hate sex, at least on TV.

I prefer a serious, sober, puritanical approach.

But then came Little Joe and his big one, and when you have one that size, one everyone is in awe of, well, you have to pause and admire it.

We were at the PNE, not finding anything. The cameraman, John McCarron, and I were hunting, and we were trying to impress a student who was tailing along with us. We wanted to show how, with imagination and insight and experience and a touch of genius, you can find something interesting in almost anything.

But we were failing. Despite there being twenty thousand people at the fair, we could find nothing that day that was different from any other day. So I said, "I got a call about a giant zucchini in a restaurant on Granville."

"But so what?" I added.

Everyone has grown a giant zucchini at some time or other. All you have to do is grow an ordinary-sized zucchini and wait. Also, it helps to water it.

"I don't want to do a giant zucchini," I said.

"Well, why don't we just look at it?" said John. "Maybe they are chopping it up into a giant salad."

So reluctantly I admitted defeat at the fair, knowing that the student would learn nothing and would go back to school and say, "Those guys are no good. I could do better."

We drove to the Normandie Restaurant, an old family establishment at 10th and Granville. We walked in, and right inside the door on display was a zucchini about five feet long.

"That's a big zucchini," I said.

A woman customer, who was on her way out as we were admiring it, said, "Joe has the biggest one I've ever seen."

Then she smirked and left.

"I told you it would be a good story," I said.

On camera, we asked women and men inside the restaurant about it.

"Big."

"Really big."

"Biggest I've ever seen."

Each answer was followed by a smile.

Then Joe came out of the back of the restaurant. Small. Really small. Maybe five foot two, maybe not.

"He has the biggest one of any man I have ever known," said a woman, drinking tea while looking at Joe.

"I wish I had one like that," said a man.

Joe picked up his zucchini, put it over his shoulder and walked around his restaurant, showing off his large one.

"Could I touch it?" asked a woman.

Joe accommodated her.

"That's mighty impressive," she said.

After a while it got too heavy for him to carry, so he put it back on the counter at the front of his restaurant.

"I'm glad you're not showing it off any more," said a woman. "I was tempted to ask you if I could have a nibble."

We left.

"What just happened?" asked the student. "We didn't cover that in school."

"Sex," I said. "Beautiful sex. Tempting sex. I love sex on TV."

"But it's just a man with a zucchini," he said.

Wrong. It was a man walking around his restaurant talking to patrons. It was interviews with men and women commenting on something the man had that was magnificent, incredible and unbelievably large. It would be a TV audience smiling as they heard people say what every man wants to hear and every woman lies about.

And it was only a picture of a small man with a giant zucchini.

The student said, "That's twisting the truth."

"The truth," I said, "is what everyone watching wants to believe."

Six months later the restaurant burned down. That was sad. But by then, the zucchini had gone into many dishes and had been happily shared by many, a fate that is only to be envied.

Northern Building Supply

It started with a microbus covered with stickers. More stickers and decals than I had ever seen. Stickers that said "Don't Mess with Texas," and "Peace Now," and "Eat Beef," and other things, mostly clean.

It turned into the Bonanza Creek of stories.

That sounds silly. What the heck does "Bonanza Creek of stories" mean? It is a cliché. Except that it was true.

That microbus was the first nugget in the gold pan. But just what the heck is a microbus? Unless you were alive in the sixties or early seventies, you don't know about the microbus. It was not a mini van. It was a cultural revolution. It was freedom at fifty-five noisy miles an hour. It was an expression: Get in your microbus, paint a flower on the side and go to San Francisco. On the way you listened to the song "Convoy," in which Rubber Ducky talks to Pig Pen as they form a convoy of trucks across the country. In the middle of the long line of tires and CB radios is a microbus with eleven long-haired friends of Jesus, meaning hippies. If you had hair down to your shoulders during the sixties and seventies and had friends, one of them had a microbus.

And Brad Bradfield had one too. He was an immigrant from South Africa. Never had I met someone so funny and inventive and outgoing. Brad was a leftover hippie who loved meat.

He had long hair and a microbus plastered with decals, literally covered, with a funny horn and a squirt gun on the side. He had driven back and forth across the States and Canada and Mexico. But mostly he had these stickers. I was doing a story on stickers, and there was his microbus, just covered.

"Do you want to see my skateboard?" he asked.

"No, I'm happy with your bus for now."

Brad worked in an old cow barn on Borden Street, one block east of the Knight Street Bridge. Yes, an old cow barn. And there began a relationship that turned into one story after another, and stories are like gold, and this place was overflowing with it.

Half a block from Brad's barn is a lumberyard called Northern Building Supply. One afternoon a cameraman and I were inside the yard, at the edge of the Fraser River, taking pictures of the water. He was shooting under the bridge when a sailboat came motoring in. It docked, and a guy stuck his head out and said, "Hi. Bet you don't know what we're doing."

He was right. But that is what is so beautiful about life. No one knows what anyone else is doing. We live in non-stop mystery stories.

"We're sailing around the world with our parrots," he said.

He showed us inside his sailboat, which had little room left for human sailors. Mostly the space was taken up by cages filled with the birds that once were the pets of pirates.

"We want to be the first people to sail around the world with the birds we love."

That was story number two.

Story number three happened when I walked back up Borden Street and found Marilyn Wild, who runs a tool rental shop a quarter block from Brad's cow barn and his sticker-covered microbus. Marilyn also grows vegetables in a back-alley garden, right next to a shop that rebuilds alternators. She cultivates fresh tomatoes and basil next to worn-out cars. So I asked if we could do a story about her.

"May I ask, how old are you?"

"Sixty-nine," she said.

Her work is knowing about heavy-duty chisels and road-paving equipment. Her work is also moving some of that stuff around an ancient shop.

Her work makes her hands dirty and her fingernails chipped and her arms tired.

"Why do you keep working?"

"Because if we didn't have this, my husband would have nothing to do. I have my arts and crafts, but he has worked hard all his life. He can't leave this."

Theirs is not a plan taught in business schools. The profit margin is slim. It is the faithfulness margin that keeps the tool rental shop going. The big box stores have ground places like it into the dust.

Marilyn's husband was seventy years old when I met him. He came back at that moment with an old piece of equipment. Her face brightened up.

It was just past the middle of February, and she said she had made him a Valentine's card and a cake. She had done that every year since they had been married.

How long?

"Forty-nine years," she said. "Fifty coming up."

Then she smiled, and he kissed her cheek.

You want to visit a tool rental shop where the love is stronger than the hammers and drills they have on the walls, go to Northern Tool Rental on Borden Street. You may not need any equipment, but any holes in your heart will be fixed.

The next nugget from the lumberyard was LT's Diner. It was like one of those forts that you build when you are ten or eleven. Your hideout is solid, but the roof is low, and squeezing in and out through the narrow door is a challenge. At LT's Diner, you walk up crooked, narrow steps and go into a room where the roof is barely high enough to clear your head. The tables slope just a bit and the menu is simple: eggs and pancakes and burgers and sandwiches.

The LT stood for Little Tony, who was Chinese from Saskatchewan and cooked everything but Chinese food in his diner.

"We did not have that in Saskatchewan," he said.

I did a story about Tony, and then Tony retired. He sold his business to a writer from California who was not doing so well as a writer and decided to move north with his Canadian wife.

Her name is Lucy and his is Tim. So the place stayed LT's.

The oddest thing about Tim is not that he was a writer who couldn't sell enough of his words to keep eating, but that he had never cooked—not anything—before he bought a diner. The first omelette he ever made was in his own restaurant, while a customer with a beard and heavy, sawdust-covered work clothes gave him instructions across the counter.

So I did another story about LT's, just a slice of life about a restaurant with a low ceiling and a smiling new cook who had added one thing to the dining experience: a comment book on one of the tables.

"Good omelettes. Good burgers."

What could be better for a chef who was just learning to cook? Tim showed those words to us so proudly you would have thought he had just sold a new novel.

Eating at one of the tables at LT's was Bert Thomas. He started a small lumber business at a time when he hauled his own wood from the mills, stacked it himself and then delivered it. He did not have enough money to take a day off. Now Bert owns the whole yard, which stretches for three blocks. He also owns most of the buildings on Borden Street, which runs up from the yard to Southeast Marine Drive.

Every person who rents a space from Bert in his yard or on the street, whether it's for a workshop or a garage or a tool rental shop or an old cow barn or an illegal living space, says Bert is the kindest man in the world. He gives everyone a break. Everyone who is honestly working to make a living knows Bert will charge him or her less rent than they would find anywhere else in the city.

By charging less, Bert has become rich. Every day, and I mean every day, he eats at LT's Diner, which under the new owners has become LT's Café. And every day Bert orders a grilled cheese sandwich and fries. The meal is not supposed to be healthy. Bert doesn't much care what he is supposed to do or not supposed to do. Until he fell off a ladder a couple of years ago, he hadn't missed a day of work in more than seventy years.

Before the accident Bert rode a bicycle around the yard and did fifty push-ups a day. Now he walks with a stoop. But he still goes to work and still eats grilled cheese and fries and still undercharges his tenants.

You want to meet him, go to LT's Café at lunch.

That's what Frank Aicken did. Frank started Sperling Lumber when he was a young man, and he wanted to meet Bert, who had started Northern Building Supply when he was young. So Frank went to LT's Café on a day when it was pouring outside. He climbed the old stairs and ducked through the low doorway and slid up a table that was slanted to one side. If Tim ever served meatballs, which he doesn't, they would roll off the plate.

Frank ordered a burger and fries. Every morning for breakfast, Frank has bacon and eggs.

"How old are you, Frank?" I asked.

"Ninety-one and a half."

"Ha," laughed Bert, who had just arrived for his lunch of grilled cheese and fries. "I'm ninety-two."

The two men sat at the table and talked of trucks in the days when a transmission was a thick chain that looked like it came off a giant's bicycle. They talked of working fifteen hours a day and doing their calculating on the back of brown-paper lunch bags.

Frank started his yard after the war, when he wanted to build houses but could not get nails or boards. There were shortages of everything, so he started his own yard to supply himself.

Bert started his yard long before that, when he was out of work and needed to do something.

These are the kind of men who have made this country a strong, independent land. They needed something and filled the need themselves. They did not ask for government support or tax credits or handouts or incentives or special consideration. They just did it.

Frank retired in his fifties when he was bought out by another yard. Then another yard bought that. Rona is now the name over the yard he started. Bert still works. His rolltop desk is covered with papers and invoices and letters asking him for the secret of his success. If they have to ask, they'll never get it.

After lunch the two of them walked down the long stairway, each encouraging the other to be careful. Outside the rain had stopped. They held each other by the arm and walked off together between the piles of cedar and hemlock. Forklifts detoured around them. They were in no danger. Everyone respects where Bert walks, and when he walks with a friend the way is always clear.

Both men had canes, Bert because he is stooped, Frank because he is almost blind. In the yard were a dozen men and a few women wearing work clothes. All know the lumber business, and they knew they were looking at royalty. In silence they watched as the two old guys walked and talked and talked and talked. They were like teenagers who had just met and found a soulmate.

One day we walked up Borden Street toward the sticker-covered microbus to look at Brad Bradfield's skateboard.

Brad has dedicated the last ten years of his life to making the wildest board in the world. He's designed it so that the wheels at the back are in the normal position but those at the front are placed in a row like on in-line skates.

The model can be manoeuvred like a surfboard, hence his company name, Surf-On-Shore. The company has two employees, Brad and his partner, Jason. Brad builds the boards from scratch, using cans of fibreglass. He has gotten patents and then gone broke trying to get people interested in buying his boards. After years of frustration and shattered promises, he is starting to have some success.

To make a living while his skateboard business is getting off the ground, Brad barbeques ribs and steaks for parties from another microbus he turned into a portable smokehouse. One time he was so broke, he rented out a large walk-in closet in his home inside the barn to someone else to live in, when the other guy was having even harder times. Bert keeps Brad's rent low so that Brad can keep working on his skateboards.

And there is Walter, who runs Walter's Auto Fix-It shop a few steps farther along Borden Street. Walter is a tough manly mechanic who drives a pink Cadillac. "Why not?" he says. "It is fun."

It was a hot summer day when I was visiting, and it was Walter's birthday. But what Walter does on every hot summer day, whether it's his birthday or not, is that he waits for the ice cream truck to come along and buys twenty dollars' worth of pops and cones from the gaunt-looking guy who drives around all day ringing a bell and trying to make a living in a business where you can't get rich.

"He needs the money," Walter said.

And then Walter visits all the workshops along Borden Street and gives out the ice cream to Marilyn in the tool rental shop and to the guys repairing car radiators and to Brad and Jason and the South Asian guys working in the sweaty little wooden shack where they are rebuilding alternators. If you are working on that street any day in the summer, you will get an ice cream from Walter.

But on Walter's birthday they gathered, and they were waiting before he got there. They were waiting with "Happy Birthday" sung in as many keys as there were workers. Only one woman's voice was in tune. But then one of the South Asian guys sang him "Happy Birthday" as it's done in India. Walter did not know the words or the tune, but the tough, old mechanic was sniffing when I looked, and I don't think he had a cold.

There were more stories from the Northern Building Supply neighbourhoods. Among the boats tied up in the river behind the lumberyard, I met a guy fixing the engine on a log-salvage boat, one of those tiny but powerful vessels that prowl the rivers and bays looking for maverick logs they can lasso and pull back to the herd to collect a fee. The guy had been a business writer before 9/11. When the World Trade Center towers came down, so did his job. He started a new life. He and his wife sold everything they had and bought a sailboat to live on and the salvage boat to make a living.

"It was the best thing that ever happened to me," he said.

And there were also Daryl Luster and Jim Williams, who worked together in a shop in the lumberyard making fine furniture. I knew it was fine because the sign outside said "Luster's Fine Furniture." But Jim smoked and Daryl didn't. Daryl wanted Jim, who was his friend, to stop. Jim smoked three packs a day, which they say is not good for you.

How do you get someone to quit? Well, you tell them to quit, right? Wrong. It depends on how you tell them.

One day, on the bathroom wall next to their shop, Daryl wrote: "Lung Cancer. Emphysema."

"Those are harsh words," said Jim.

The next day Daryl wrote: "You might burn down the building and cause us all hardship."

"I didn't think of it that way," said Jim.

The next day: "Your breath will be better. Food will taste better."

"Are you trying to tell me something?" asked Jim.

This was as much like graffiti as when someone scratched the Ten Commandments on a couple of stones.

The next day: "You could burn down your house and kill your family."

"I wouldn't do that," said Jim.

Daryl said nothing, but the next day: "It kills brain cells."

"I'm trying," Jim said.

Next day: "It ain't pretty."

Jim no longer smokes.

It worked better than nicotine patches.

When you meet characters with humour you don't need a beer at night. Outside of Vancouver's parks, that lumberyard is my favourite place. It is the bonanza that kept me employed for years. I have done almost thirty stories about the yard and the people along Borden Street. And the neat thing is, you can go down there now and find many of the same characters. The microbus with the stickers is still parked on the street, near the pink Caddy. LT's Café is still serving the best omelettes in town on the most slanted tables, and Bert is up there with his grilled cheese and fries at lunchtime.

There was the truck driver, Brian Hart, who was jealous of the people who worked the lumberyard's main office. They were dry and warm while he was wet and cold out in the yard, so he used some of the lumber that is stored everywhere in the yard and built himself an office where he could stay warm and dry between deliveries. Over his office he put up a sign that said "The Boss."

"I feel better now," he said.

And I didn't mention Frenchie, who works at the pool table company across the street from Brad's skateboard shop. Frenchie balances anything and everything on his nose. He will put a pool ball on top of a pool cue and hoist it up on the bridge of his nose and keep it straight up without hands and still talk to you about the weather. He will do the same thing with an open knife, but it's hard to watch that without feeling your skin tighten.

Spend a couple of hours on that street, and you will go home with stories for a month.

Elephant Crossing

It happens to everyone who drives into North Vancouver. And it happens because of a fluke, like most things in life. But first, what happens?

"What was that?"

"What was what?"

"The deer crossing sign."

"I didn't see any deer crossing sign."

"It had an elephant on it."

"You're crazy."

Try it yourself. Drive along Mount Seymour Parkway, and I'll bet you a nickel someone in the car will say, "What was that?"

"What?"

"I swear that sign had a camel on it."

"You're crazy."

"Slow Down. Deer Crossing." Those are the monotonous words that drivers don't see on the uncountable signs on which they are written. We don't see the words because they are on uncountable signs, and who is going to read a sign that is the same as the one you just saw down the road, especially since no deer jumped out in front of you anyway.

But you do see those words in North Vancouver because between the

"Slow Down" and "Deer Crossing" is a picture of, wait, that's not an elephant. This time it's a hippo, or a camel.

What's going on? Is this a college joke?

"Slow Down. Deer Crossing." Now it's a rhino.

It was too much. I had to find out who was filling the streets with large animals.

Inside the North Vancouver District works yard, where everything looks the same, I found Cameron Stewart, who was making things look different. He was like Dr. Seuss, creating his own world outside of everyone else's.

"I just want to have fun," Cameron said. "And I want people to see the signs."

Some of his signs have no pictures, just words: "Attention Dog Guardians. Pick Up After Your Dogs. Thank You." And below that: "Attention Dogs. Grrrrr, Bark, Woof. Good Dog."

"It works," he said. "There was much less left behind after that sign went up."

Why? Because you read it and think, maybe I should pick up after my dog.

To protect a cultivated plot of dirt filled with tulips, Cameron created a sign that says: "This bed is for flowers only. Go jump in your own bed and let sleeping dogs lie elsewhere."

Feet and dogs disappeared from the flowers for the same reason that the ground got cleaner around the Grrrrr, Bark and Woof sign. People read the words.

Cameron is an artist, a writer and a comedian employed by the municipal government. Isn't that impossible? When you work for government, you give up your personality, right? You toe the official line. You do what is asked of you and nothing else. Individuality? Never!

Unless you are Cameron Stewart of the District of North Vancouver. He has changed the daily lives of those who live there. He has given them laughter and signs that truly do what they are supposed to do: get noticed.

"Oh, Dear. Slow Down. Deer Crossing."

"This Flower Bed Is in Metric. Please, No Feet."

But the funny thing about this is that Cameron did not know what he wanted to do with his life. He loved being a mechanic. He wanted to fix machines. He wanted to tinker and make things work. But he also wanted to be an artist, maybe a writer. He wanted to create things. He wanted to tinker with images and make them work.

Art? Mechanics? Art? Mechanics?

He got an offer for a great job in the world of mechanics. That should have settled it. Except that it was raining and he was sitting in his old Valiant at the corner of Oak and 26th Avenue waiting for the light to change and staring past the wipers at the vehicle in front of him. It was an old Volkswagen van. He glanced at the licence plate. "379 ART." Or was it "728 ART"? Or "ART 239"?

"Actually, I can't remember the numbers. But how could I go into machines when the licence plate in front of me was telling me to do something else?" he said.

He took some art courses, but he wound up working for the municipality. After all, you've got to eat. He started playing around in the sign shop and he produced something funny, and for some amazing reason he was allowed to bend the rules and regulations of government and his signs went up.

There were some complaints.

"How dare you spend my tax money on frivolous, stupid, idiotic signs," someone called in.

I hope that person does not live next door to anyone. He would make a miserable neighbour.

But mostly there were compliments and congratulations for having something bright and happy to read on the way to work.

"In a world where everyone is looking out for number one, who's taking care of number two? Pick up after your dog."

If Cameron had not seen that licence plate, tens of thousands of smiles would never have been born. And a smile is a terrible thing not to have. Thank you, Cameron. Thank you, licence plate.

A Pint of Guinness

In Ireland it is called a parish priest. Black in the glass, white foam on the collar. Or a blond in a black dress. Or simply a Guinness.

For much of the last century, it was the world's best-selling beer. If you like Irish-type beer, you must love Guinness. If you like German-type beer, Guinness is like black water. It has no fizz.

I like Guinness. I like the idea of drinking the working-man's brew. I like the taste. I like the buzz you get after just one, because one is a pint and by the time you finish it you feel good.

I hate to promote alcohol because it is bad for you, but Guinness is good for you. I know that because it has the second most influential and smartest advertising slogan in the history of the world. The first is "Drink Coca-Cola." In some advertising book I read that "Drink Coca-Cola" is the world's most profound slogan. It tells you exactly what to do with the minimum of words.

It was on the sides of hundreds of thousands of vending machines for decades. It was displayed under the smiling face of a woman inside half a million soda shops. It worked. Outside of jazz, Coke is America's most influential export ever.

But we are talking about the number-two spot in that book: "Guinness Is Good for You." That slogan influenced millions who would have been happy drinking milk but saw that by ordering a pint of stout their lives would be better. So they drank Guinness.

I first saw a sign advertising Guinness when I was seventeen and sneaked into the bar on the corner of the New York street where I lived. The legal drinking age was eighteen, but I knew from my friends that the bartender was forgiving so long as you sat at the end of the bar in the shadows and would slide off the stool and disappear if a cop came in. The bartender didn't care where you went, but if you were caught it would mean his licence, and so you would have to just disappear, poof.

I had an escape route planned through the toilet and out the window. Drinking was so romantic.

But up on the wall I saw a sign that said "Guinness Is Good For You." I was barely away from Coke and milk and I liked things that were good for me, so I ordered a Guinness.

"Are you sure, kid?" asked the bartender.

"Sure I'm sure. By the way, what's a Guinness?"

"It's bitter, black and awful."

"Good," I said. I didn't want to look like a wimp while I was underage and sitting in the shadows.

I had two sips, then left the bar and went across the street and drank a Coke. Guinness kept me from becoming a teenaged barfly.

Forty-five years later I was touring the Guinness brewery in Dublin. I couldn't wait to get to the end of the tour and have a Guinness in St. James' Gate where Arthur Guinness had started the whole cultural experience. I had seen the abandoned potato farms with the tiny stone huts that had been home to my ancestors. It was a brutal time. I weep when I read about the starvation in Ireland. Mass death in Africa has nothing on the Irish. But that was then, and now I was fat and healthy in the brewery that makes the world's most famous beer. And there I learned the four most important things about Guinness, at least to me.

One: The dark brew was once called porter because it was the cheapest beer, from the bottom of the barrel, and was drunk by the porters of England, the men who carried everything that belonged to others.

Two: Arthur Guinness announced in 1759 that he was going to brew this barnyard swill commercially and leased a small warehouse outside of Dublin. The owners of the land laughed at him and were so sure he was going to fail they gave him a lease for 9,000 years for £100 and an annual rent of £45. He would owe them the money forever, they figured. That lease is now behind glass on the wall of the brewery.

Three: Arthur Guinness wanted to add some lift to the label and asked his staff for help. One said it was a stout beer, meaning it was strong. So they called it a stout porter. Soon porter was dropped, and Guinness became a stout, the adjective becoming a noun.

Four: The second largest Guinness brewery in the world was built in 1936 just outside of London.

That last one was sort of interesting. I already knew that in the 1930s the Guinness family had bought land in West Vancouver and called it the British Properties because most of the folks they hoped to sell it to were British. The Guinness family built a bridge to get people there, the Lions Gate Bridge. And then they built the first shopping mall in Canada to keep people there. I knew all this, you know all this, so what's new?

What's new is that when I read the next line in the history of the Guinness family, I understood everything there is to understand.

The Guinness brewery in London was in an area called Park Royal. That is why they named the shopping centre Park Royal, to make the people who bought houses in the British Properties feel at home.

"Guinness Is Good for You" was not the only stroke of genius that that company had.

Bullfighter's Brew

"You have to find some ethnic stuff," said Keith Bradbury, my boss.

It was 1984, and the upcoming world's fair meant we would probably have some new foods in Vancouver.

"Ethnic?" I asked. "In Vancouver?"

You'd never know it now, but at its best, Vancouver back then had badly cooked British food. White Spot was fancy dining. White Spot and Nick's Spaghetti House were the number-one and number-two places to go. There were the hotels, which everyone joked had army mess sergeants for cooks, along with a few remaining restaurants on East Hastings, like the Only, which then had super-good fish and no bathroom.

What could I do for ethnic? The city was mostly white. I found three places: Hon's Won Ton House, the Himalaya Restaurant and Joe's Café.

You might be thinking: Hon's, the big Chinese restaurant on Robson. No. Hon's, the fingernail-sized won ton house on Main Street. It had three booths with seats that once had padding. Now when you sat on them your chest was even with the table. There were also four stools at the counter. You could order numerous dishes at Hon's, but most people just said, "Give me a bowl of won ton." Sometimes won ton with barbeque pork. Sometimes won ton with noodles. On a cold and wet day it was good when you had the shivers.

There were only a handful of restaurants in Chinatown then. Some were famous because you could bring your own wine or whisky, and the old slots under the tables where you could slide your bottle were still there from Prohibition days.

Hon's was the only won ton house with a specialty much like cat fish was in the southern US. Chinese soul food.

I walked in and asked if we could do a story about them.

All I remember is that a woman named Mrs. Ip, who looked like she had worked hard all her life, said yes, but we could not leave the counter. No pictures in the kitchen, no interviews with the staff, which totalled five, and no pictures of her daughter.

Mrs. Ip and her husband had opened the steamy soup restaurant only two years before, taking over another old restaurant that had been there. She was working long hours to send her little girl to school.

The result: The little girl studied hard, went to university and grew up and took over the soup kitchen with a Canadian gusto. The massive Hon's dining room on Robson is all chrome. The waiters, both the men and the women, wear black suits, white shirts and ties. The kitchen is open, revealing a culinary ballet with noodles and chicken flying up and down, in and out of pots, choreographed by clean-cut, athletic cooks.

And now I cannot even begin to think of Hon's as ethnic. A while ago my wife and I were in Hon's on Robson and saw a young man and woman sit down near us. He placed a small candle on the table and lit it.

You can't do that, I was thinking.

Then he said something to her and took out a small box and opened it. She smiled and nodded.

He took a ring from the box and put it on her finger and they held hands and stared into each other's eyes. Then he blew out the candle and they ordered dinner.

They were South Asian.

The second place was the Himalaya Restaurant at 50th and Main. Can we come in? Can we look in your kitchen? Can we pry into your lives?

"Sure," said Kewal Pabla. "As soon as I check with my brother."

His brother showed up.

"Can we . . .?" I asked.

"Sure, as soon as I check with my brother."

His brother showed up.

"Can we . . .?"

"As soon as I check with my brother."

Four brothers who came to Canada to find they had no jobs and not enough money to buy houses. What to do?

They pooled their money and bought two houses at 49th and Main, behind a gas station, then knocked them down and built one of the first mega houses in Vancouver. It was 4,000 square feet in size, one of the first super houses in the city. At the front was a big living room. The two wings, each two storeys high, had four bedrooms on each floor. Each of the brothers took a section with four bedrooms.

I was in that house. I never saw so many kids playing in one living room in my life. All of them were in heaven. Cousin after cousin after cousin to visit as soon as you rolled out of bed. But according to city bylaws there could only be one kitchen in the house. I saw four wives with one mother-in-law sharing one kitchen. Oh, woe. I left, with prayers for each of the wives.

The restaurant they opened a block away thrived and was one of the first East Indian restaurants that drew large numbers of non–East Indian diners. That was back in the days when we said "East Indian." Now we say "South Asian" and most are happier, even though it is the same people and the same food.

Now the Pabla brothers own half of that street, including a fabric store and a travel agency and the restaurant.

And what else has happened: the last story I did about them showed three generations of Pablas singing Christmas carols around a Christmas tree and a plastic Santa in their restaurant.

The wives and mother-in-law joined in with the Punjabi version of "Merry Christmas." They had not only survived, they were smiling.

Canada put some magic in their lives.

And then there was Joe. Joe is Portuguese.

I knew Joe's coffee shop had the best cappuccino in town. I knew that because it said so in a giant scrawl across the window: "Best Cappuccino in Town." Inside was Joe, making coffee.

"Can you make me a cappuccino?" I asked.

He pointed to the sign and looked at me like, duh. You order a cappuccino, you don't have to ask if it can be made.

I remember the milk foam growing taller and taller until I thought it was riding an elevator.

Joe had been a bullfighter in Portugal. He was at the top of the league. Then a bull tilted his head just below the cape Joe was holding and shoved his horn into Joe's stomach. The bull lifted the young man in fancy clothes over his head and the horn dug in deeper.

A news photographer took a picture of the man impaled on the horn of the animal. It was a prize-winning photo, and the photographer was thrilled. The crowd screamed as crowds do when the thing they say they are not waiting for happens, like a crash in a car race or a fight in a hockey game or a goring in a bullfight. Everyone got their money's worth, except Joe.

A professional bullfighter who loses to a bull is out. Another chance? No. It is not like a goalie who lets in a puck. After the hospital Joe was out of the ring and on a ship with the thought of heading for Mexico and the third-string bullfights down there. But how do you get to Mexico? His ship was sailing to Canada because one of his brothers was there, working in construction in Montreal, and he said he could get Joe a job to help pay for the trip.

Life is a series of strange connections and absurd coincidences. The only reason you exist is that meeting between your mother and your father when they were both single and they spotted each other in a bar or at church or the office and talked and at some point got naked and had a passionate affair. They were not thinking of you at all, but along you came. If either one of them had been sick that day or missed church or turned around to order another drink at the bar before their eyes made that beautiful connection, you would not exist. The same with Joe: it was a fluke. He had a brother in Montreal. After Montreal he took the train west, to be closer to Mexico. From the train station he walked through Vancouver and wound up on Commercial Drive.

The street was dimly lit and seedy. Joe walked south from Hastings and passed the Portuguese Social Club. He heard his native language. It was comforting. Two storefronts later he passed a coffee shop that had a "Help Wanted" sign. That was 1972. He thought he might as well work for a little while before going on to Mexico.

He never left.

"This is my family," he said, looking at the collection of Commercial Drive misfits with nowhere else to go who sat for hours at his tables with empty cups in front of them, and at the men in suits who were buying and selling million-dollar properties at the next table. The businessmen and women knew that this was a part of the Drive where their word would be believed. Joe's was honest. There were pool players, occasional drug dealers. Once a politician ran his campaign in a corner of the shop. And there was the most famous incident, the love-making lesbians.

Joe tolerated everyone. You did not need to buy coffee to sit in his café. You could study at a table all day or watch television without paying. You could hold hands and smooch regardless of your sexual preference. But then came the day when some lesbians got into heavy petting at one of the tables. The petting grew more active. They were on top of a table. Joe asked them to cool it. They said their civil rights were being violated and organized a protest in front of his shop.

For several days the women against men picketed in front of Joe's Café. I am not talking about lesbians in general. Most are sweethearts, most are wonderful. My favourite woman couple is two ex-nuns I met during a gay pride parade. They have been together for twenty-five years. I am referring to the militant women of Commercial Drive in the eighties who just for fun would grind up men for breakfast and so they put a picket line in front of Joe's door. Business was down. The police said they had the right to picket. But Joe was a bullfighter. He had faced horns; he would not back down against the women. Late one night he installed a sprinkler system under his awning. The next day, when the picketers returned, he turned on the water.

"You can't do this," they yelled. "It's against our civil rights."

The police said Joe could do this.

Protest versus sprinkler. It took a few days, but the protesters wilted.

Joe never went to Mexico. Every year he said he would go back to Portugal for a visit, but he never did.

"I have to watch my family," he said.

He never married. He took over the night shift. He worked until midnight or one in the morning. He closed only when the last customer left. Then he was back again at 8:00 a.m., shopping for coffee and milk and buns and cakes. During Expo '86 he could see the lights of the fair from his window, but he said he could never take a day off to go.

Along the walls in Joe's Café are black-velvet pictures of bullfighters. Few customers ask why they are there.

When I did the story about him back in 1984, his brother, Tony, who had come up to work with Joe, played the part of a bull. He crouched down low, and with his fingers up by his head, he charged toward Joe, who held a dishtowel out like his old-time cape. Tony raced in as Joe stepped aside gracefully, like a bullfighter. No, like a ballet dancer. Joe was professional and the best. Tony went by without touching his brother.

Joe had a stroke one night in 2006. Luckily he was at work, and when he collapsed the medics were called. They were right around the corner. He spent months in rehab. In the spring of 2007 he went back to Portugal for the first time in thirty-seven years. He met a woman he knew as a girl when he was fighting bulls. They are now writing letters to each other.

Joe is back in his shop and the painted words in the window still say "The Best Cappuccino in Town." You don't argue with a bullfighter.

A Fast Game of Cricket

I grew up playing baseball. I grew up with nothing but baseball. When I was a kid in the 1950s, baseball was the only sport. We street urchins had never seen a football game. Despite New York having a major league football team, we knew nothing of football. We knew they used a funny-shaped ball, but we did not know what they did with it. None of us could afford to go to a football game, and even if we could have, someone would have said, "Why are you wasting your money on football when baseball season will start in only seven months?"

In school, we heard that soccer was a sport they played in Europe where they had to run for ninety minutes and hit the ball with their heads. They could not use their hands. We could not imagine such a thing. We always used our hands. We were tough, but we could not run for ninety minutes. Those Europeans must be supermen, we thought. Beyond that, we had no idea what soccer was.

We had never seen a basketball game. Despite New York having a major league team, we did not know how the game was played. They had a basketball in our school, P.S. 54, which the teachers tried to get us to bounce. We thought that was dumb. Girls bounced balls. Boys threw them. So we stole the basketball. We tried to play with it on the street one night, but failed. It was not like baseball, and baseball was the only thing we understood.

We often sat on the sidewalk outside the bar on the corner of our street, underneath the elevated train. In the summer when the door was open, we could see the ten-inch black-and-white TV at the far end of the bar. It always had baseball on. We knew baseball. It was the only sport. We played it with rubber balls and broomsticks, or with hard balls and gloves when we got lucky and got a glove for Christmas.

When I grew up, I heard about something called cricket, supposedly the grandfather of baseball. Like, yeah. You think I'm going to believe that baseball came from anywhere except the hand of God, given to the early American people as a gift? Baseball was invented just as it is; it did not evolve from simpler life forms. To think anything else would be heresy. Baseball was pure. And like apple pie, and wars, it was American.

And then I came to Canada and went to Stanley Park and saw a game of cricket. It looked like a game for sissies. The players used a funny-shaped bat. They did not wear gloves, obviously because the ball was soft. The pitcher did a dance before he threw the ball, and all the players had the same uniforms, and there was some kind of scoring system that looked like an Einstein theory before it ran out of space on the blackboard.

I decided to do a story on how silly cricket was, and the players played along. Despite all the rules of this game, they liked to laugh at themselves and it seemed as though they did not mind if someone else laughed at them too. I shot the story with Ken Chu, a cameraman who has shared many of my stories.

"I don't understand what they are talking about," he said to me after we talked to the players.

"It's okay, Ken," I said. "I don't understand either, but I know it is not as good as baseball, because baseball is the only true sport in the world."

He looked at me like I was a bigoted fool and a narrow-minded idiot. He is very good at picking up details.

"Baseball is much tougher than this," I said.

One of the players shouted to us that we better not stand so close. We might get hit.

"It's okay," I said. "I play baseball. No ball is going to hurt me."

It was right after that someone hit a ball and it went backwards. The only balls that go backwards in baseball are foul balls, and they are stopped by a strong wire at the backstop.

There is no backstop in cricket. There was just me standing right in the path of the ball. It's all right, I thought instantly. I play baseball. I can catch the ball, even if I don't have a glove.

The ball was coming at me at two hundred miles per hour. This is going to hurt, I thought. Actually, I didn't really think that because I didn't have time to think anything. I didn't have time to move out of the way of the ball. I only had time to feel it go into my shin and drive the pain up through my leg and out through the top of my skull and then continue up until it exploded somewhere north of heaven.

"Ow, Jesus, God, ow, ow, that hurts," I said, very loudly.

"Sorry, chap," said the player who had told us to move away. "That happens all the time."

Later, when I wiped away the tears enough to continue interviewing, I held one of the balls they were playing with. It was much harder than a baseball.

Bigger bat, harder balls, no gloves. No gloves! That was like early baseball. Harder balls. That was like early baseball too. I knew this because after that cricket game I read up on early baseball. I read that baseball grew out of cricket. And that cricket is played in streets and back alleys in the Caribbean and in India and in England by ten-year-old kids without gloves. What the heck was I thinking in my baseball bigotry?

I bow to the grandfather of baseball. In his white uniform, the cricket player is one tough guy. You can watch a great game almost any Sunday at Brockton Oval. It's a nice change from baseball.

Up on the Roof

"**W**ould you drive around the park again?"
"Again?"

"Yes, please. Maybe we missed something."

That was me asking and cameraman Steve Lyon wondering why. We had driven around Stanley Park on a gloomy autumn Sunday, and no one was out. There were no tourists, no cricket players, no photographers, no fishermen, no gardeners, no lovers. There were no eagles, no harbour seals, no cougars, no rabbits, no police horses.

"Why do you want to go around again?" he asked.

"Because I don't want to go downtown again," I said.

We had already scoured downtown, and there was no one out. It was a gloomy autumn Sunday, as I said, and most sensible people were still in bed or having coffee and reading the papers. There was no reason to be out. There was no sun, no snow, no cool breeze or warm breeze. What person in their right mind is going to go out on a rotten, gloomy day unless they have to walk their dog? And long ago I learned that unless the dogs are walking on their two front legs with their tails pointed straight up, I am not going to stop and ask their owners anything.

"Hello, I hate to bother you, but is there anything unusual about your dog?"

The beam in their faces shines light over my muddy shoes.

"My dog? Of course! My dog is the best. My dog can do anything. My dog can catch a Frisbee, and one day my dog woke me up by licking my face. I realized I had slept in and I would have been late for work if it wasn't for my dog. Would you put him on television? I paid $600 for him at the breeder, and I love him so much."

That is why I don't talk to people walking dogs. But I do ask cameramen to drive around the park again because no matter how many times you look at something, you can still sometimes find something interesting if you look again.

"Wait. Stop."

"What do you see?" he asked.

Up on the roof of the Prospect Point coffee house I saw someone sweeping. Well, you can't pass up someone sweeping a roof, can you? Just think of it: he's sweeping.

"So what?" said Steve. "There are leaves on the roof. It's autumn. Leaves fall in autumn. He's sweeping leaves. I repeat, so what?"

But he's a person, and he's breathing, I think. Those are two main requirements for stories.

We stopped, and I shouted up to the man with the broom and asked if we could join him on the roof. He nodded.

Okay, why does someone want to come up on the roof? He is thinking he owes us money. No. He doesn't owe anyone money. We are government agents. No, it is Sunday and government agents are sleeping. We are lost tourists. That must be it.

Steve and I see a ladder and climb to the roof. I do not like this. The ladder is not well balanced. And besides, Steve's right. What are we going to get, other than a man sweeping leaves? Everyone sweeps leaves.

At the top I say what I always say: "Hi, we don't want to bother you, but we are from Global Television. Can we take a picture of you?"

The man on the roof says, "Why do you want to take a picture of me? I'm only sweeping leaves."

"Well, it's neat," I lie, hoping he has a story and knowing that leaf sweeping on top of a roof will not make the six o'clock news.

"Okay," he says, "but it's boring. I'm just sweeping leaves." He tells us his name is Tony.

He sweeps and Steve shoots and Tony and Steve are both right. It is boring. Boring doesn't make for exciting television.

"Do you watch the ships?"

The roof is at the edge of a cliff, so you can see ships go back and forth under the Lions Gate Bridge. It is beautiful. A ship is going by right now.

"No," he says. "I hardly notice them."

"Do you like the animals in the park?" I ask.

"No," he says. "I hardly notice them."

He is sweeping. He is a man intent on his job. Nice, but I will have to climb down the ladder and go on looking for something to save my own job.

Then someone else's head appears at the top of the ladder. It is a dark, handsome head.

"Hello," I say.

"Hello yourself," he says. "What are you doing here? I am the manager of the restaurant."

I explain and he says he will not call the police. His name is Richard. Then he says he has to change the flags on the roof. They are ratty. The flags are the symbols of British Columbia and Canada.

"Are you going to do that now?" I am anxious, desperate, and see a possible way to hold onto my job.

"I could," he says. "They're in a box downstairs."

Please, please, please, I beg silently. "Where you from?" I ask, because he is dark and handsome.

"Morocco," he says.

Then another head appears at the top of the ladder. It is someone with a box in his arms.

"He's from Israel," says the manager on the roof.

Morocco, Israel, Arab and Jew. Putting up flags in Canada. Thank you.

"Our dishwasher's from Chile," he adds.

Thank you again.

"Do you want to talk to him?"

My eyes are wet. Do I want to talk to him? Do I want a winning lottery ticket? A close second is talking to someone from Chile next to someone from Morocco next to someone from Israel.

"I wouldn't mind," I say.

The manager bends over the roof and shouts down to the Chilean dishwasher. He comes up the ladder.

"Are you really from Chile?" I ask. I ask probing questions.

"Yes, they were nice, they gave me a job." He is referring to the Arab and the Jew.

The manager speaks up again.

"And our waitress, she's from Mexico."

Oh God, oh God. Is sex this good?

Soon she is up the ladder, and we have four people from four countries and they are all putting up new Canadian flags. Could any picture be better?

And over there with his broom is the non-communicating roof sweeper.

"He's from Argentina," says the manager.

I do a head jerk. A double take. How good can things get? Five countries, even if the fifth doesn't talk much.

I ask, though this is forbidden, "Can I get you to do something? Can you sing 'O Canada'?"

Yes, and they do and life is wonderful. Five countries together under one flag. This is a wonderful nation. It welcomes others and they become new people called Canadians.

They finish the song and I am happy and we are leaving.

"Wait," says the man who is sweeping the roof. "There is something else."

Please, I think, don't stop us. I am out of time. Time is killing me. It is three o'clock now and it is an hour's drive to the TV station and then fighting to get an editor and then two hours of editing and writing and the six o'clock show starts at six o'clock, but of course, please, tell us your story.

"It started in 1955. I was born in Argentina."

I know that, I am thinking.

"And I had a happy childhood."

Wonderful. Please, stop.

"And then my father died."

Sorry.

"And my mother couldn't bring us all up."

Sad.

"My mother had too many kids and not enough money."

Everyone has that problem.

"And then I was adopted by a Canadian family."

Interesting, but I have super-good friends who were adopted and that is not such a dramatic event.

"And then I came to Vancouver looking for work."

Steve, I am thinking, if you are still shooting this, please turn off your camera. I am not going to go through all that tape for nothing.

"But I could not find any work."

Are you ever going to wrap this up?

"So I came into the park and thought my life was over. I was sleeping in a pile of leaves next to this coffee shop when Richard found me."

Richard, the guy from Morocco.

"He brought me in and gave me coffee and a job."

Richard put his arm around Tony's shoulder.

"We are all family here," says Richard.

Oh my God, I am thinking. I don't know how this happened, but this is what the country is, or is supposed to be. Kindness, diversity, pride, work. I am also thinking, at this moment I am the luckiest person in the world.

"Thank you," I say. We turn to leave and they give us one more chorus of "O Canada." A Mexican, a Moroccan, an Israeli, a Chilean and an Argentinian singing one song on one roof next to one flag over one coffee shop.

"Steve?" I ask.

He smiles. He did not turn off the camera, not for a second. He is much better at getting stories than me.

Stories are like socks. Just because they were not in the drawer the first time you checked doesn't mean they have won't jump back in there before you check again.

Rodney and Raymond

The morning I got the news about Rodney's death I was in a bathroom and kitchen renovation shop. My wife wanted the bathroom renovated. I was happy with the 1962 style we already had.

"What wood finish would you like on your cabinets?" asked Archie, the renovating guy.

"How do I know?" I said. "My wife knows things like that."

"I have to know soon," Archie said, "because we have to order the finish and it will take six weeks and we can't do the reno without the cabinets and your wife said she wanted this done as soon as possible."

"Excuse me," I said, "my phone's ringing."

Of course my phone wasn't ringing. It was vibrating, which I like the feel of very much, but it always seems rude to reach for a phone that no one can hear without an explanation. So I say my phone's ringing. It adds a touch of mystery.

"I've got some bad news for you," said Clive Jackson. He is the assignment editor at Global News, meaning he is the most important person in the newsroom. He decides which stories get covered. There are other most important people, too. Like Dale, who assigns the cameras and says to Clive, "No, what you want is impossible." So Dale is sometimes the most important person in the newsroom. And there is Karen, who assigns the editors, without who no story would be put together. So Karen is sometimes the most important person in the newsroom. And then there is Randy, who decides which stories wind up on the air and says to Clive, "No, you have too many stories to fit into sixty minutes. We will have to drop some." So sometimes he is the most important person. And there is Luizs, who answers the phones. If she didn't do that, nothing else would work. So often she is the most important person.

But that morning the call was from Clive, who is my boss. Since it was my day off, I knew it had to be important.

"I've got some bad news for you. I wanted to tell you before you hear it from anyone else," he said.

Do you know how many thoughts go through your head when you hear that? I've been fired. The station has changed its name again, and I will have to get a new jacket. Someone has died.

"Someone has died," he said.

Well, at least I wouldn't have to find a new job or get a new jacket. But immediately I felt bad for thinking that.

"I heard it this morning from Derek," Clive said.

I had done a story about Derek the week before. He drives a giant front-end loader for the Park Board. Usually he works on the beaches keeping the logs in neat order. He is a friendly guy who loves Manchester United, his hometown team. Everyone told me not to ask about Man U because, well, I would be sorry.

I was too stupid to take their advice. I asked, and the entire interview was about soccer, including the first Manchester United game Derek saw in 1958 when he was eight years old. He still remembers the score. He remembers that Man U lost. He says he will get over it someday.

Derek had called Clive to ask him to tell me that Rodney had been killed the night before, by a coyote.

Rodney was a rooster. It was a hot summer day when I first saw him wandering around the maintenance yard of Stanley Park. He was big and proud and reddish, and he was cock-a-doodle-dooing. He had been adopted by the gardeners, who had found him starving at the far end of Pipe Line Road, which is the road in the park that takes you to the miniature railroad.

The railroad, by the way, was created after the huge typhoon named Freda levelled part of the forest in 1962. "What are we going to do now?" some park officials said after Freda. "It's devastation. It is the end of the park." Then someone suggested building a miniature railroad where the trees had been. It turned out to be one of the best attractions in the park, so thank heavens for destructive typhoons.

Back to Rodney. He had suffered the fate of many small animals that are brought into homes as pets before it is discovered that they don't behave like dogs or cats. They don't come when called. They will not be housebroken, and the floor gets very messy. So the disgruntled owners take their pet chickens and roosters and rabbits, many, many rabbits, especially after Easter, to the park and let them go, thinking they will have a wonderful life. Instead they are hunted down by coyotes, chased, scared half to death and then chomped into eternity. Home was never like this.

The gardeners who found Rodney brought him back to the maintenance yard, where they built a little shed for him to escape the sun. They brought him food and played with him, as much as you can play with a rooster. In their annual staff photo they gathered around him. making sure he was in the middle of the picture. He went from scrawny to fat and healthy and strong and arrogant, just what a rooster is supposed to be.

We put that first story about Rodney on television.

Then came the winter, and one day I was looking around the maintenance yard again for something interesting. I had already done a story on the shoe tree, which is wonderful. You should go to the yard and look at it. It is a tall metal pole, and every gardener who retires from the park hangs his or her boots on it. There are countless pairs, covered with moss and filling with rain and swinging in the wind. There is no fancy scroll showing the gardeners' names. There is nothing that costs the taxpayers a penny. There is just a pole hung with muddy, worn-out boots, which is the way gardeners prefer to be remembered.

I looked for Rodney again, but he wasn't in the yard where the gardeners worked. Many of them don't work there in the winter, and maybe the handouts were getting slim.

"He's ours now," said a policewoman who was riding by on a horse.

The mounted police squad keep their horses in a stable behind the gardeners' section of the yard, and they had adopted Rodney for the winter. They'd built a perch for him that stuck out from one of the horse stalls. He was warm and secure inside the stable. He wandered free and safe around the horses. The police fed him, they talked about him, and then they changed his name. He was now Jerry because there was an episode on *Seinfeld* about a rooster.

That was story number two about Rodney who was now Jerry.

Then came the summer again. It was late in the day, and I was getting near the point of being desperate. That is when I say, "I can't do this job any more. I am too old to be hunting for something quirky every day. I must look like an idiot. I am going to quit." And then I look through the windshield and say, "Story god, HELP, please."

After that I say to myself, "We will find something." And I really believe that. When you really believe you will do something, you do it. It just happens. It is not that you change reality, but you change your perception of reality. Somehow you are able to see things that were there before but you missed them.

I went to see my old friend Rick Harrison, a gardening supervisor, who had told me about the ashes and the Nine O'Clock Gun. (You'll read about that later in the book.)

"Tell me something new," I said.

"There's nothing left to tell."

This is not the way the story god is supposed to work. I started to leave, dejected.

"Oh, I forgot," he said. "We got Jerry back from the police and he is Rodney again and now he's got a mate."

Wow, I thought. That will be so romantic, so sweet. And so quick to do, which was good because by now it was even later and the clock and the story god were racing each other. But Rodney and his chicken lover would make the news. Thank you, story god.

"But his friend is Raymond," said Rick. "Rodney is gay."

"Are you kidding?"

Rick shook his head. "We don't kid about things like that."

We found Rodney and Raymond behind the gardeners' office. The two of them were preening and clucking and wandering off together.

It is good to get a second opinion, so I went to see Bonnie, the pole-dancing gardener. She does her dancing after work, and she gave us a demonstration once on a pole holding up a stop sign inside the park. She was fully clothed, including her work boots, but she slid up and down on that steel shaft in a way that made me not want to blink. We put it on television and had ninety seconds of either pure family-values exercise or erotic TV, whichever you wished to see.

"Of course he's gay," she said. "But it's perfectly acceptable. This is the West End."

It was true as far as we could see. Rodney and Raymond did everything together: ate, slept and wandered off into the woods. Raymond was another orphan, abandoned by some good people who knew that if they just opened their car door a little, no one would see them throwing him out before they sped off. They never would think of themselves as bad people. Bad people are always others.

Story number three on Rodney, now joined by Raymond.

When I got the phone call from Clive about Rodney becoming a coyote snack, I was sad. I went back into the reno store and thought, "Rodney would just go straight ahead and pick the colour he liked."

Bless him. But I am wiser. I brought home the samples to let my wife choose.

Turtles? What Turtles?

It is lovely in the summer to go to one of the city ponds and watch the turtles. They are there by the hundreds climbing up on rocks and on each other, soaking in the heat and simply having a wonderful day.

Turtles? There are no turtles in British Columbia. Not the way nature planned it. But then, what does nature have to do with the way we fix things?

They are like the grey squirrels, which are everywhere. However, grey squirrels are not native west of the Rockies. They never made it over the mountains. Until we meddled with nature, only black squirrels existed in British Columbia. But after Stanley Park was created some wise man said, "We should make this a world-class park and import some grey squirrels, which are famous in Central Park in New York." So they put in an order for a dozen. Those twelve happy transplants have left behind twelve million descendants.

Speaking of Central Park, when it was created some wise man said they should have living there all of the animals that are mentioned in Shakespeare, to make it a world-class park. So among the creatures they imported were half a dozen pairs of starlings. Those twelve happy immigrants have left behind twelve trillion descendants, which have moved right across the continent and swarm through the sky like locusts, driving out native birds.

Perhaps we should shoot all the wise men.

Back to turtles, which according to the Chinese are very lucky. This I learned from Tommy, who is a gardener at the Sun Yat-Sen Garden. Kindly parents take home some of the palm-sized, hard-shelled green things for their children so that they will have good luck.

And then the turtles grow, much faster than the children.

"So they bring them here and let them go," said Tommy.

Of course non-Chinese do the same thing, with roosters and bunny rabbits.

Turtles are released in the pond at the entrance to Granville Island and in the pond at the pitch-and-putt golf course in Central Park in Burnaby and in Queen Elizabeth Park. In fact, they are released almost everywhere there is water.

In the winter they take one last big gulp of air, then swim down to the bottom of their wet Canadian homes and go to sleep under the mud. In the spring they rise with the sun and take a deep breath. They have few natural enemies, and they eat almost nothing but bugs and weeds. And they are a lot of fun to watch. So far the turtles in British Columbia do not seem to have altered any great natural plan, but that is only so far.

I once did a story about a couple from southern California who had just come back from a cruise to Alaska. They saw no whales or bears or eagles. I guess it rained a lot on their cruise. But when I met them they were happily taking pictures of the turtles in the pond on Granville Island.

"This is great," they said. "We don't have any of these at home."

And then they went off and spent some more money.

Obviously, the turtles were lucky for them, and for us.

Weight Loss Guaranteed

"**B**oy, you're looking good," I said to Ken Chu.

Ken and I have worked together for thirty years. He carries the camera, he does the hard work, and I take the credit. I feel bad about that, but that's where it ends. If I could take a picture, I would be doing his job because there is a lot of talent in photography.

Together we have been treed by a grizzly bear (get my first book), and we have seen the swastika man take off his shirt for us (see elsewhere in this book), and I have watched Ken get violently seasick while we were on a practice rescue mission that turned into a real rescue in a storm off the west coast of Vancouver Island.

I know him pretty well. And every day that I have known him, he goes to Chinatown to eat, and he eats too much. Like many of us who eat too much, the meals turned into ounces, which turned into pounds, and the pounds turned into new pants and larger jackets.

We have all said, "I'm going to lose weight this year. I failed last year, but this year for sure. But first I'll order that plate of pasta or chow mein or barbeque ribs with fries. But only today, not tomorrow."

So when I noticed that Ken had lost some weight I was complimentary, but mostly I was jealous.

"What did you do?"

I expected an answer involving the Scarsdale or the Steveston or the Beijing diet, expensive things so you eat less. Or else he had joined a gym, which I try to avoid because they make you work and I do enough of that at home, with the dishes.

"My daughter," he said.

In that nanosecond before he continued, I imagined he would say, "My daughter has put me on a vegetarian diet, which I hate, but I will do anything for her and so I am losing weight."

And in that nanosecond I knew I would not go on a vegetarian diet for anyone, not even myself.

Then he continued. "My daughter got a dog."

All at once I understood, just as you understand.

My daughter came home with two cats once.

"Can I keep them?"

"Of course."

Then she left home.

We had the cats for almost ten years while she lived in Europe.

"Your cats are doing fine," I wrote to her.

"I've got another one here," she wrote back.

"That's nice," I wrote.

But cats are not like dogs. And Ken's daughter had gotten a dog.

"And you take it for walks," I said to Ken.

He nodded, a healthy but sheepish nod.

"She promised she would walk it every day and I would never have to do it," he said.

But then he told me his daughter often had places to go and people to see and she had asked if he could take her dog out, just this once. It became a daily walk. Then twice daily. He would get up early to take the dog for a long walk along the river in Richmond and as soon as he got home from trying to make me look good on television, he would take the dog for another long walk.

He didn't wait for his daughter to ask. He was having fun. He had never had a dog before, and he was talking about it with increasing fondness.

"I have fun with him. He does tricks. He loves me."

Then he said the words that really made me hate him.

"I've lost thirty pounds," he said.

He didn't change the way he ate or drank. He just took his daughter's dog for walks. I did a story on his weight loss, and I got more phone calls and emails on that story than just about anything else I did that year. Other news may be more important, but most of us just want to look and feel better without killing ourselves to do it.

Forget the gym. Forget the diet books and the resolutions and the lies you tell yourself about having just one piece of chocolate. Let your child get a dog, and make sure he or she promises to walk it every day or else. Guaranteed, you'll start losing weight the next week.

The Curve in the Road

You are driving west on Highway Number One, as if we have a highway number two or three. Don't kid me. But shortly before you come up to the 200th Street exit, there is a curve in the road and you go around an old stump.

What the heck is that stump doing in the way? Why don't they blast it? Why don't they remove it? Why don't they make the highway straight so I can hurry up and get to where I'm going?

I got a letter from a little girl named Lisa who was in grade four. She said she passed that tree when her family drove to see her Nana in Hope. "Why does the road bend around it?" she asked.

I did a story that said:

Dear Lisa,

In 1916 Charlie Perkins was a young farmer who was holding onto a plough as it cut through the earth. The plough was being pulled by a horse, and it is not easy to hold reins around the back of your neck while you have two hands on the plough and the horse is going faster than you can keep up with. Charlie's farm was in a place few had heard of called Langley. He had heard about the war going on in France, and though his family did not want him to leave, he had decided that he would finish the ploughing for the season, then climb on his horse and take the day-long ride to Vancouver and join the army.

Charlie was bright and had some schooling, and he wound up in the air corps as a pilot. After staring at the backside of a horse, he was now staring at the backside of a propeller and gunning an engine that took him into the sights of enemy fighter pilots. He was one of the very lucky ones. At the end of the war he went home to his farm in Langley and went back to his horse and his plough.

But many of his friends did not. No one who goes to war comes home the same person as when he left. In World War I, Charlie's war, the death toll was horrendous. With a population of less than eight million, Canada lost 60,000 soldiers, almost twice as many as in World War II.

Sit in a pew at Christ Church Cathedral, on the left-hand side about three-quarters of the way back, and look at a plaque on the wall. It lists the members of that church who died in World War I. You will still be reading when the service is over. And that is just one church. The same happened in every small town in British Columbia. Go to the cenotaphs in any of them and read the names. You would hardly believe the town had that many men.

Charlie had lost many friends, and he wanted to do something for them. So on his remote farm he planted a tree, a cedar, and said that as long as it grew, his buddies would be remembered.

Time passed. Vancouver was growing. Langley was growing. The country that Charlie had fought for was booming, and people need-ed a way to get around. Horses would not do anymore. Everyone was driving cars, and in 1950 the construction of the fabulous Trans-Canada Highway began.

Right in the way of it was Charlie's farm. He was paid for the land they took away. That was fair. He did not argue, even though he knew that he would have to cross a highway to tend to half his farm. He did not complain. But then he saw the surveyors laying out the road, and it was aimed straight at the tree he had planted for his friends. More than forty years had passed since he planted it, and it had grown into a mighty memorial almost ten storeys high and so big around that when his nieces and nephews played hide-and-seek they disappeared behind it. Charlie had nailed a few plaques to the tree to commemorate his friends. The tree also wore a metal Canadian flag.

And then came the bulldozers.

Charlie stood in front of them. The construction crews told him to move. Charlie did not budge. The road foreman told him they would be back the next day with the police.

Charlie showed up the next day with a shotgun. They could take his farm, but not his tree.

The police, being wise, backed off. The standoff went on for several days, with Charlie sleeping at the base of the tree with his shotgun in his lap.

The news of the standoff at the tree went to Phil Gaglardi at his office in Kamloops. He was the Minister of Highways. He was known as Flying Phil because he had so many speeding tickets. He was a short, tough guy who looked more like a teamster union organizer than a politician. I was doing a profile of him one day in his office when he told me that every day at lunch he took off all his clothes and ran around his office naked, to get the feeling of freedom. He also exercised a free mind.

"I got on the phone and told the foreman, 'Don't be an idiot. Go around the tree,'" Gaglardi said. "The foreman said it would cost extra. And I said, 'Those men paid with their lives.'"

And so the road builders redesigned the highway and made a bend in it to save the cedar.

And what do you think happened then? Some vandals, which is a nice way of saying some rotten kids who should have been sent into the trenches of World War I or the foxholes of World War II, used gasoline and set fire to the tree during a drunken stupid party in the woods and killed the living monument.

Lisa, when you get older and some of your friends want to do something stupid, tell them about the tree. Maybe you can save them from hurting someone else.

Anyhow, since the tree was dead, the top of it was cut off. The stump remains, and the road still bends around it. If you stop at the pullout there, you can see underneath the vines that have grown over them the plaques with the names of Charlie's friends.

The only reason I found out about that tree, Lisa, was because you asked. Thank you, Lisa.

The Frozen Affair

L ike many affairs, I never saw it. Thousands of others, no, millions of others never saw it either. They looked like a friendly, happy foursome out for a day of touring. They stopped to take a picture, and you suspected nothing.

One of guys, with his old Instamatic, was snapping the other three, his wife and the other couple, their best friends.

"Hey, get a little closer together," he said, and he motioned them with his free hand to squeeze up tight. He held his camera up to his eye. He did not know what was going on under his nose, right in front of his eyes, and neither did I.

I saw them nearly every day back at Expo. They were on the fairgrounds, snapping the picture, all smiles and happiness. I would walk past them and think, what a lovely group, and what realism. This was 1986, and they were dressed like they were living in 1986, slightly flared pants, casual jackets, matching sweatshirts for one couple and matching sweaters for the other.

Even though they were bronze and never moved, it was obvious the two on the right-hand side were married because they had on shirts that said, "Great Adventure, Jackson, NJ." And the woman on the left was for sure married to the guy taking the picture because they had on the same style of sweater, plus they had matching wedding rings. She also had a curious, delighted, almost surprised look on her face. I figured she was enjoying the fair. And she probably loved the way her husband was taking the picture.

The other woman, who was on the far right, looked a smidge annoyed, but I thought I was just reading that into her face. She was probably in a hurry, and the other woman's husband was taking too long to get the picture. So much like a man to want to organize everything and get everyone to stand just right. Besides, they had enough pictures. The fair had gone on for 180 days, and he had been taking the same picture for 180 days.

Nice statue, I thought, very realistic.

Then the fair ended and the statue was moved to Queen Elizabeth Park, up near Season's Restaurant. I saw it standing there for years, in the rain, in the sun, in the snow, the same guy taking the same picture of his wife and their friends.

I saw the statue while I did stories about the smog covering the view of the mountains; I gave out postcards to tourists so they could see what they were supposed to see. And I saw it after we did a story on the talking parrot in the McMillan Conservatory, that glass dome at the top of the park where it is summer all year round. The parrot did not talk while the camera was running. And I saw the statue when we did a story on the Japanese tourist who got off the tour bus dressed as a cowboy. His group had been to Calgary, and he wanted to change his life. Now he had a Stetson, a sequined shirt, tight blue jeans, a gun belt and holster without a six-shooter, and beautifully tooled cowboy boots. Everyone else on the bus was dressed in matching blue suits.

But I never *knew* about the statue until I overheard a tour guide from Brazil telling her group to walk around the back of it. She was speaking in Portuguese, so I had no idea what she was saying. I only saw the group walk around the back of the statue, pause and stare. Some smirked, some gasped, most laughed. Some couples on the tour moved apart as though their own personal secret had just been exposed.

I asked the tour guide about it, and in English she said, "Don't you know? I thought everyone knew."

"Knew what?"

"What's going on there."

She took me around the back of the statue that I had seen hundreds of times and pointed out the right hand of the man who was married to the woman on his left. Not only was his right hand fondling the rear of the woman on his right, the woman who was the wife of the man taking the picture, but his ring finger was, well, it was up in the crack between her cheeks, partially hidden by the folds of her skirt but not completely.

"My gosh," I said. I had never noticed.

Suddenly the sculpture, which was entitled "The Photo Session," came alive. Suddenly there was a story, a scandal, hanky-panky. Suddenly it was a novel, a play, a motion picture with friends and cheating and passion and an ending that had not yet been written.

No wonder the woman with the surprised look on her face had a surprised look. Maybe it was a smile. And no wonder she was squeezing really tightly against the man on her left, resting her left hand on his shoulder. Her right hand was behind her back, holding a couple of his fingers while another finger did its probing. No wonder the wife at the other end was just slightly pulling away from her husband. Wives always know when something is up.

And that poor dummy with the camera, who was trying to squeeze them together, had no idea it was not just the film that would be developing.

How did I miss it? How much else have I missed? If you went to Expo, did you see it? Or if you have gone to Queen Elizabeth Park and seen the statue, have you noticed the affair that has lasted longer than most marriages?

And the biggest question of all: What happened next? When he got the pictures back did he notice that his friend's arm was descending much lower than his wife's back? Did the wife at the far end notice the same thing? Did either of them ask? Did they hear lies? Were there screaming hissy fights and divorce, or was it all over by the end of the day, when the two who should not have been doing what they were doing came to their senses?

Check out the statue and make up your own ending, and if you are with your significant other, make sure the ending is just what she or he wants to hear.

Paradise Island

I was standing on a concrete road-divider straining my neck to see my twin sister. The road divider had been dumped off far from a road. It was poking out of the edge of a clump of blackberries.

"Be careful," said Dave McKay, the cameraman. He pointed to the brambles on one side of the slab of concrete, where the thorny vines were thick and went from slightly below my feet in a long jump down to the Fraser River.

"Don't worry," I started to say, but I did not get out the second syllable of "worry" before I lost my balance and fell backwards down the slope and into the thorns.

That had something to do with toast with peanut butter always falling butter-side down. I could have fallen on the other side of the concrete and stuck out my foot and been totally fine. But no. With a fifty-fifty chance of doing something intelligent, many of us pick the thorny side of life.

"Oh God, oh my Lord, oh heavens, it hurts." I think I also said something stronger.

Luckily Dave had brought along his strong twenty-year-old son, Dylan, to ride around with him for the day, and the two of them waded into the brambles to pull me out. Without them there is no way I would have gotten home that year.

I was scratched and sore, just like my kindred spirit, my sister, who was tied up in the river below. I still wanted to get to her. I thought I heard her calling.

We were at the eastern tip of Mitchell Island, which is under the Knight Street Bridge. Sometime shortly after the earth was created the island had trees and grass growing on it. A small community lived peacefully there, a short rowboat ride away from Vancouver to the north and Richmond to the south.

Then came the bridge, and a change in zoning, and now the island from one end to the other is covered with junk cars and concrete plants and scrap-iron yards and shipping containers and more junk cars. Boats are built there, cars are crushed and tourist facilities are limited. There are two diners that serve only breakfast and lunch.

A handful of ships and boats are tied up at the eastern end of the island. One of them is Motor Vessel *Bowie*, my sister. She is 136 feet long, made entirely of wood. She once had a crew of thirty, but now is home to two.

Greig Thoriaclus, who says he is descended from the Vikings, bought MV *Bowie* for one dollar. How do you manage to pay one dollar for anything? Even the dollar stores charge more than that. But this boat was lying on its side and half-sunk. The owner wanted to get rid of it.

MV *Bowie* had served out the closing years of her life in unglamourous jobs along the West Coast. Over the past half-dozen years, Greig had put his life into her, as well as every penny he earned. He and his girlfriend, Tana Frie, turned her from a useless water-filled hulk into a romantic floating fairytale palace. The interior decking is all new hardwood that Greig got for free because the pieces were mismatched. The galley is cozy. From the hot tub on the top deck, there is a view of the stars and the river. The tub, like the boat, is heated by a wood fire that burns inside a large steel firebox. The *Bowie* is beautiful inside.

I first met Greig when I discovered his boat on Mitchell Island and found him decorating a Christmas tree inside. He loves Christmas. He said on Christmas Day the year before he got the best gift ever. His birth mother called him out of the blue from Whitehorse.

"I knew it was her from her first words," he said.

I didn't know anything about why he and his mother had been separated.

I did not ask and he did not tell. I only knew that when he told me about her call he was sparkling, and that was good enough.

He said that when he told her about the boat he was living on being old and sunk and waterlogged, she replied with motherly concern, "Holy (bleep)!"

"That's my mom," he said proudly.

On the shore next to where Greig's ship is tied up is a two-person factory making boxes.

"Hey, I know you," I said.

It was the same couple I had met behind Northern Building Supply, across the river. They had the sailboat with four parrots inside and they were planning to sail around the world.

But Linda and Neil Lunney never did make that trip, mostly because Neil was a house builder and while they were still planning their voyage the truck with all of his tools and equipment inside was stolen.

"We were devastated. We still had bills coming in," said Linda.

They were left only with a table saw and a drill press and a bin of scrap wood.

What they did was look at what they had and start making small, fancy boxes out of the scrap wood. The boxes were elegant, carefully joined and sanded. And then Linda sold some to a company that wanted something to package their specialty coffee and teas in at Christmastime. The first order was for one hundred boxes. The second was for one thousand. They had to hire people to keep up with the demand.

Then they started using wood from pine-beetle–killed trees, wood that no one else wanted because it was stained blue. In boxes it became a work of beauty. They now have orders flooding in and boxes pouring out.

Someday, when they have time for a vacation, they will probably take that long boat ride.

And next to them on the island I met a Chinese immigrant who worked alone in his sheet-metal shop. Often immigrants who initially don't speak English and who work alone retire with little understanding of the language. Not Weitang Chen.

He put a radio in his shop but did not tune in to a Chinese-language station or music. Instead, he turned on CKWX, all news all the time. He knew everything there was to know about crime, politics, sports and the weather, and he practised his new language with the traffic reports every ten minutes. "My teacher," he said, pointing to the radio. "CKWX has taught me to speak very fast with short sentences."

I said good-bye.

He said, "Tomorrow will have 90 per cent chance of sunshine." Then he added, "In case you wanted to know, the Canadian dollar is up four basis points today."

There were other stories around Mitchell Island. There was the junkyard cat, and the woman who worked in the junkyard office but at lunchtime put on boots and hunted through the piles of rubble and twisted remains and collected the vases and clocks she found.

And there was Jim Dorsey, who bought demolished cars from ICBC, fixed up the bodies in his shop and turned them into anything the movie companies wanted. A Ford written off in Vancouver became a New York or a Boston police car. A worn-out Canada Post truck became an ice cream truck or an undercover surveillance van. Few of the movie vehicles ever needed to run. Most of them were smashed or overturned or driven off a cliff, or else they were parked on the street in a scene that helped the movie look more authentic and made Jim a bundle of money.

Jim's story is like all success stories. He got an idea and he did not put it in a drawer and forget about it.

He was working in a forklift shop painting forklifts. The chances of advancement, he said, were not large. But he knew how to paint a metal body and he watched movies and saw that the main props in many stories were cars, especially ones that got stepped on by elephants or got stuck on railroad tracks. And he knew movie companies were flooding into Vancouver.

Jim started with four cars and one can of paint. When I met him, he had eighty cars, trucks and fire engines in the shop. Few of them were causing any air pollution because few of them would start. But they all looked like the real thing. They were just waiting for a camera and an explosion.

But I always go back to the old wooden ship tied up at the eastern tip, MV *Bowie*, my soulmate. The reason: It is a former US Navy submarine chaser, built in the Brooklyn Navy Yard in 1944. I was conceived and later born just outside the Brooklyn Navy Yard in 1944.

The ship served in the navy during a war but never saw any violent action. I served in the air force during a war but never saw any violent action. She found her way to Vancouver, I found my way to Vancouver. She is looking a little worn, but still has some life left in her. I am looking a little worn, but still have some life left in me.

I look at that ship and say, "You and me, kid, we'll see how long we can keep going."

But the best thing about the old sub-chaser is something Greig said after showing me around her.

"I believe in magic. You put your wishes out there, and sometimes they come true. But you got to believe." The ship was his wish. His girlfriend was his wish. Hearing from his mother was his wish.

You can see the *Bowie* from across the river at the south foot of Victoria Drive, or close up from the eastern tip of Mitchell Island. But to do that you have to stand on a concrete road-divider that is surrounded by blackberry bushes. Be careful.

It Takes Guts to Build a Steam Clock

O n any summer day, just before noon, several busloads of tourists are dropped off at Water and Cambie streets.

"That's it. That's what I've been waiting to see."

They all say that as they get ready to watch the world's most famous steam clock toot its steam-driven time checks.

How do we know it is the world's most famous? Well, because it was the first one, and all other steam clocks in the world are based on it. Yes, that is true.

The tour guide is speaking and the cameras are coming out and there is total attention being paid to the one object in Vancouver that is photographed more than the mountains, more than the totem poles in Stanley Park, more than Smart cars that are everywhere in Vancouver and nowhere in America.

"Hurry, Marge, get the camera. It's almost noon."

"I'm trying. But it's stuck under the raincoat. Why did we bring raincoats? We were told it was going to rain here, but it never does."

Of course not. It's August. It doesn't rain in Vancouver in August. It is hot and beautiful. Wait there it goes: "Toot." The steam clock is going toot and Marge hasn't got her camera out.

"We're missing it," says Marge's husband as they stand there looking at it.

"Toot, toot, toot." Twelve times. They finally get their camera out and take a picture on the last blast of steam and say, "Darn, we missed it. We missed the other toots." A month later they will say, "Here is the famous steam clock, but we missed most of the tooting. We heard it, but here's a picture of its last toot."

"What a shame," their neighbours will say. "I would have loved to see the other toots. What did they look like?"

"Just like this, except more."

"Such a shame. Missed them, huh."

"No, we heard them, and they sounded neat. Like, it went 'toot, toot, toot,' twelve times. But we missed it with the camera. Marge never was good with the camera. But here's a picture of me with the clock behind me, except it's not tooting."

"Shame."

Now go back to 1975, and the city bigwigs are strolling through Gastown. They want to make the area into a showcase. They want to do something with it that will bring in tourists and get rid of vagrants.

One of them passes a steam vent coming out of the ground.

"What can we cover those things with?"

"Planters?" says one of the bigwigs. "Put big flower pots over them."

"No, they'll get filled with litter."

"How about a clock? The Birk's clock is neat. We could use another one here. It would be a steam clock."

That is how it happened. It was a momentary slip of the tongue, putting together steam and clock.

"Where do we get a steam clock?" asked a bigwig.

They looked around and saw a watch repair shop a few steps away. The whole group of city officials walked into the shop, where Ray Saunders was squinting into the back of a watch.

"Can you make a steam clock?" the officials asked.

They did not wait until Ray had looked up from his work. They just blurted out their official-status question.

Ray looked up. These were clearly people to take note of. They had attaché cases, that being back when attaché cases meant you must be important.

"Steam clock?" he thought in the half-second after their official-sounding question. "Steam clock? Why, I have never heard of a steam clock. I have no idea how I would even start such a challenge. I wouldn't even have the foggiest idea of where to begin."

So he answered in one of the great moments of bravado, "Of course I could build a steam clock. When do you want it?"

Right then and there the officials gave him the contract to make a steam clock, which neither they nor Ray knew would be the first steam clock in the world.

Ray had learned watch fixing in high school from an old teacher. The activity seemed to fit the young student perfectly. He was quiet and studious, and watchmaking would be a good career. Ray fixed watches for other students and teachers and then went to work in the Woodward's watch department before going into business for himself.

His life was tame and quiet before that day when the officials walked in and he opened his mouth and said yes to something he knew nothing about.

He wrote to famous and established clockmakers in England, asking how to build a steam clock. They wrote back saying that he was crazy. They said that no clock could operate on steam, that it would rust out and clog up and he should give up the idea before he ended up like a broken main spring. That was back in the days when watches still had springs that broke.

He wrote to more clockmakers, and eventually one sent him the plans for a steam clock that had been made a century earlier but apparently did not work very well. They cautioned him that he was attempting something equivalent to creating a sun dial that would work at night.

Ray spent the next year and then into the following one tinkering and trying and trying again. Endless frustrating late nights later, and after a visit to that old high school teacher, who gave him some ideas, he produced the world's first steam clock that actually worked.

It runs on pulleys and levers and steam, and it toots four times an hour. The clock mechanism is electric, but the steam is real, and it is triggered by the clock. Since then Ray has travelled the world, building other steam clocks in shopping malls in Japan and the US.

He works in the basement of his home in north Burnaby, and he is still quiet and shy. But he is also the world's most famous maker of steam clocks. It is not such a bad idea to occasionally say yes to an impossible task.

The Lone Soldier

Every November 9 the city's park workers start cleaning the cenotaph on Hastings Street with high-pressure hoses. They dig the moss out of the cracks in the pavement and wash the benches and power-blow the paper cups and heroin wrappers from the curbs.

The drug dealers start moving away from the park because there are too many people around who are actually working. A few years ago the park workers removed all the beautiful small bushes in the park because the dealers were hiding their drugs under them.

On November 10 the television stations will spend the day laying cables and setting up platforms for their cameras. They will move efficiently because they have done this many times before. The same cameras, the same platforms and cables are used whether the event is a hockey game or a police standoff or a ceremony for old soldiers.

Following that, a small squadron of officials will invade the park with BlackBerries and looseleaf folders. They will be from the city government, the provincial government, the army, the navy, the air force, the veterans' affairs department, the Park Board, the police department and the Mounties. They will be joined by officials from the sea cadets and the air cadets and the Canadian Legion.

They all get together to try to make sure the ceremony the next morning

107

will run smoothly. In truth, it is only by the grace of God that the whole thing works.

On November 11 they will come by the hundreds at first, and then the thousands. Most of them see the park only once a year. Men and women with medals, many of them in wheelchairs, will be moved to the front. The rain will fall and the bagpipes will play and the tears will come, flyovers will occur and cannons in the distance will be fired and the same speeches and poems that are read every year will turn the park into a holy place.

One year, far at the back of the crowd, so far away that all he could see were the umbrellas in front of him, stood a man alone. He was so far back he was nearly on the sidewalk of Pender Street, fully at the other end of the park.

I asked and he told me he had landed in Sicily and fought his way to Massena. He fought in hand-to-hand combat, the most ancient, bloody, terrifying thing anyone could ever face. It is the first kind of fighting that was invented, fighting with no space between you and the enemy, and killing with nothing but what is in your hand, or being killed by his hand.

The man had been wounded twice in the stomach. He was possibly an officer or a sergeant during the war, though he did not say so. He said he had had two companies that were down to fourteen men. There should have been two hundred and forty.

"The replacements would come in the middle of the night and be dead by morning. You never got to see their faces until they were lying on the ground. You took off their dog tags to find out who they were," he said.

He wore no medals, only a red poppy. When the bugle sounded in the park he stood automatically at attention. In his hand was a rolled-up umbrella instead of an Enfield.

"Why aren't you down there with the others?" I asked, pointing to the guests near the cenotaph.

"I don't have to be," he said. "I just close my eyes and I see my men."

I asked his name.

"Egan," he said, "Egan Folz. I'm German." He laughed, the kind of laughter that recognizes how ironic all of our lives become. He was born in Canada, a German-Canadian fighting Germans.

A year later I would be on the beach at Normandy, where I saw a young family playing in the sand. A mother, a father and a toddler were filling a plastic bucket. They were vacationing, the same as me. They were speaking German. It is like the American tourists who now go to Vietnam, or the Canadians and Americans who are now driving Japanese and German cars and saying they are the best. Or the Japanese, whose national sport is now baseball. If only someday we would smarten up before we kick ourselves in the groin again.

When the ceremony was over, Egan Folz said, "When I was young I thought we might lose the war if I wasn't in it." Then he shook his head at his own words. "Absurd," I imagined he was thinking. Absurd, as a young man, to think that he could change the world.

But as he left, tall and proud, I said to this German-Canadian, humble and wise hero: "You might have been right."

Oppenheimer Games

The sun rose beautifully over Oppenheimer Park. The golden rays warmed the backs of the crack dealers in the southeast corner of the park. It brightened the morning for the drunks sitting on the ground near the playground in the northeast corner. It warmed the hands of the homeless folks who had just got another handout meal from the Sisters of Charity on the western side of the park.

And then came the players, all dressed in white with their mallets and little hoops and hard plastic balls. The old Japanese croquet players had arrived for their weekly game in the same spot where they have been playing since the 1920s.

They gently hammered the hoops into the ground. Then, partly in Japanese, but mostly in English, they chose sides and began to play. They played like the Japanese play all games, with a huge amount of gusto and excitement, even though most of them were in their very late years. I was in Japan once, and I got exhausted just watching a game show on television.

They kept score on computer scoring devices strapped to their wrists. A Japanese person without a computer nowadays would seem odd. And they explained to me that this was not croquet, but gate ball. I looked and watched and it looked like croquet to me. But no matter what the name, I was watching a game that seemed like it could not be played where it was being played.

They were like a garden of bright, white flowers moving among the somewhat less bright and energetic other citizens of the park. I asked some members of the bleary-eyed audience what they thought of the contrast.

"What contrast? What are you talking about, man?" answered one who did not look like he enjoyed being called a contrast.

"'Cause they're different," said his friend, who I think stopped a verbal tirade from falling on my head. "We don't bother them and they don't bother us," he said.

And that was true. One side played with total attention and the other side watched, as much as they could keep their attention on anything.

I asked one of the players about the others in the park.

"They never bother us. They seem nice," he said.

Before most of the audience was born, this was the centre of Japan Town. It was much smaller than Chinatown, but the culture was just as strong. There was a Japanese hall, a Japanese school and Japanese stores. And there was gate ball in Oppenheimer Park.

Then came 1941, and the game ended. The stores closed. The hall was abandoned. The school shut down. And everyone who was Japanese was sent off to a camp. Many of them, while waiting to be moved to camps far in the interior, were imprisoned only a half-hour walk away in the cow barns of the PNE.

When you walk through the old buildings where you look at the horses and pigs and cows and chickens during your visit to the annual fair, try to imagine being locked up in there, in vast open rooms, because of your race. It did not matter that you were born in St. Paul's Hospital and that the only language you knew was English and that you were about to enter Britannia High School and you really wanted to join the army and fight for your country. You were locked up because you were Japanese.

Some young Japanese men did manage to leave their camps and join the Canadian army and go to Europe and die. On November 11 visit their memorial in Stanley Park, right near the back of the aquarium. Read the names of the dead, and keep reading and reading and reading. You will be there a long time.

After the war those in the camps were freed and most slowly came back and started their businesses again because this was their home and they were Canadians and this is the land they loved. And they went back to gate ball in Oppenheimer Park.

But the park was changing. Over the next few decades, especially in the 1980s and 1990s, it became an extension of Main and Hastings. Still the game went on, with dignity and humour and some really good shots over the bumpy threadbare grass. The players never asked for anything, never complained about sharing the park and never stopped playing.

As a result there has never been an incident between any of the fans and the players. And when the game that I was watching ended, the team wearing white had won. Again.

The Mary Hill Bypass Woman

When I was growing up in a tough neighbourhood in New York we heard about the beggars in India. I had never seen a beggar. We were surrounded by desperately poor people who worked two jobs and would be ashamed to apply for welfare. As for sitting on the sidewalk and holding their hands out, never. By God, shoot me before that.

Now in Vancouver begging is among the top ten new local businesses. "Travelling. Need Food. God Bless."

Go to hell. I have watched scores of you making a career out of begging. Some have been there for years, growing fatter and working in shifts, passing on their cardboard signs as the tools of the trade.

It is an easy way to make a living. Okay, it is a hard way; you have to stand out in the rain and the snow and under the hot sun. Construction workers do the same, and traffic-control women and cops and people delivering flyers. But they pay taxes.

Obviously, I do not have sympathy for most beggars. I spent years doing stories about the closing of Riverview and the schizophrenics who were pushed out of the old hospital and who should be cared for and aren't. I believe I can see who we should embrace and help and who we should stare down and say, "You bum, get a job."

The bums of life are out there saying, "Give me something." They don't add, "Because I am too lazy to work and I am doing better looking pitiful than I would be getting up in the morning and moving a broom or flipping a burger." There are thousands of empty positions that are going begging in the city. Begging on the street is a cop-out for a wasted life.

While I am on this, I must mention the classic story created by some kids at the Emily Carr Institute of Art & Design. They took a mannequin, put an overcoat over it, placed a hat on its head, slumped it down on the sidewalk on Robson Street, and put a paper cup in front of it.

The mannequin made $20 in the half hour we were filming it from half a block away. That's $40 an hour. That's $40 untaxed dollars an hour. That means a skilled mechanic would have to make $60 an hour before taxes to get the same as a brainless, heartless, plastic dummy on a sidewalk. That's absurd.

But there was also Linda, the first honest homeless person I'd met. She was known as the Mary Hill Bypass Woman.

We started getting calls in 1992 about a woman living in the bush just off the Mary Hill Bypass in Port Coquitlam. I went out to investigate. There she was. Or rather, there was a tarp like an igloo, off to the side of the road.

"Hello," I say to the tarp.

No response. I lift a corner of the plastic.

"Hello?"

"Go away."

Ahhh, a voice.

"Can we talk to you?"

"No."

I am ecstatic. "No" is a response. It is not yes, but at least the person is breathing, and that is a start.

"Can we come in?"

I am looking into the underworld of two shopping carts filled with stuff and a woman sitting between them under the tarp. It is her home.

"No."

"All right," I say.

It truly is her home. You don't go into someone's home if they say no.

We wait outside. Eventually she comes out. She looks much older than whatever her age is. She is wrinkled, her hair is matted, her eyes are tired.

I shake her hand, and her hand is dirty. She is the first homeless person anyone has noticed in or near Vancouver.

She lives off handouts from drivers who pass by. They toss her sandwiches and donuts. She is doing fine, she says.

I follow her over the next two years. She moves about along the parkway. So many people call the TV station saying something must be done about this woman and I do so many stories on her that the government in Victoria takes notice and passes a motion that she be arrested under the Mental Health Act.

She is taken to Royal Columbian Hospital, where they bathe her and examine her and say she is sane. There is nothing wrong with her. She just wants to live outside the normal world of comfort and convenience.

She moves from the bypass to the First Avenue on-ramp off the Trans-Canada. Workers nearby are worried that if a car goes off the road it will plough into her tented home.

I want to talk to her about this, and after years of getting to know her I lift up the flap of her home and poke my head in and she says hello.

She comes out and we hug. While traffic goes by and her world sits behind her and her future is unknown, we hug. It is one of the most profound and loving moments of my life. The woman who was known as the Mary Hill Bypass Woman, and who I slowly learned was Linda Black of unknown past, who lived under a tarp and kept her belongings in shopping carts, hugged me. She squeezed and then let go. You love people for different reasons, and I loved her because she was honest and did what she wanted to do.

And then she went back to her life. She asked for nothing. She wanted nothing. She got some food from passersby. She never put out a hat or a cup; she never held up a sign that said she was suffering.

Of course she was suffering. Something terrible had happened to her. Maybe many terrible things had happened to her. But she did not complain. She did not stand on a corner with a sign saying, "Pity me. I am suffering."

She lived her life as she wanted, and then she disappeared. I know she died because I felt it. I'm not psychic, but you know when someone you love is no longer there for you. She was gone. Her body was probably found by police and transferred to the city morgue. When it wasn't claimed, it would have been transferred to Mountain View Cemetery, where all the unknown and unwanted wind up. There she would have been cremated and buried in a mass grave with other unknowns.

I love you, Linda. You were the queen of the homeless. The current crop of beggars is not fit to follow your shopping cart. You never slept in front of someone else's door. You never complained. You never whined. You never blamed anyone else. When it comes to being homeless, you were a class act.

Granville Island

B ehind a Plexiglas case was a meal on a plate, steak and potatoes and vegetables. Alongside was a salad. A fork and a knife were set on either side.

It had been there for a month. And it had another month to go before
it was removed.

I am not outraged. I am confused. I am bewildered. I am dumbfounded
to the degree that I cannot express myself because this rotting plate of food
is ART.

I know it is art because it is in the Emily Carr Institute of Art & Design,
which is so famous it could knock your socks off. Many famous people have
graduated from that school, and it is named after the strangest artist ever to
live in Canada and one of the weirdest in the world.

Emily Carr was an eccentric at a time when eccentrics were a dime a doz-
en. But she stood out. She wore strange clothes and pushed a baby carriage
with a monkey inside and ran a rooming house where strange things were not
only allowed but encouraged. And she painted pictures of, of what? "Let me
look at that again, Emily. Those are trees. And totem poles. Don't you ever
paint anything else?"

"Why? I love them."

She painted hundreds and then hundreds more pictures of trees, all
cedars, and totem poles, all towering with faces in them.

"I'm trying to get the feeling of being here."

I don't know if she said that. But if you read anything about Emily Carr's life, you know she probably said something like that.

She wore a knitted skullcap and painted moody cedar trees and had to wait until she died, poor woman, to be recognized as a genius.

And then a school was named after her and the school is on Granville Island, which like Emily is a work of genius.

Long ago the island was a sandbar, hence the name of one of the restaurants on the island: The Sandbar.

"Why is it is called The Sandbar?" I asked a delivery man bringing fish in early one morning.

"I've got a load of salmon and squid to deliver, and you are giving me a test?"

I love guys like that. He did not say he did not know. He said, "Back off, fellow. You have asked a stupid question of someone who, unlike you, is actually working for a living. If your question was about the Canucks or the Lions, I would have known the answer, but not some esoteric nonsense about the meaning of a name."

At that moment, he is my hero. I grew up with guys like that. They work and fight through the day and if they survive that is the only test they wanted to pass.

So I told him.

Granville Island started out life as a sandbar where the residents, who would later be called aboriginals, dug up shellfish at low tide. It was a good life. The tide went out and dinner was served.

Then Whitey came along. Whitey built some roads and cut down a lot of trees and imported beer and whisky, but his biggest adventure was to start wars in Europe. The second one was a whopper. He invited everyone to join in and die. And during these wars, the folks who were running this country said we have to do more for our side. So they hammered some metal sheathing around the sandbar and filled it with dirt. Presto, an island.

Its first name was Industrial Island. But those who took the Granville Street streetcar to get there called it Granville Island.

By the time of the second big war in Europe you could not find a shellfish within five miles of Granville Island. The place was jam-packed with saw mills and machine shops and foundries that were filling the day and night air with smoke and flooding False Creek with pollution. By the 1950s False Creek was so clogged with gunk that the two men vying to become mayor of Vancouver both ran on the platform of filling in the waterway.

"There's no water left anyway," they said. "So let's get rid of it."

Luckily, politicians seldom keep their promises.

During World War II the island sounded and looked like a row of black-smith shops in hell. A glowing ingot of steel would be pulled out of a roaring furnace and hammered into a link in a chain. Hundreds of thousands of links were made for the Canadian navy, each of them by hand, one at a time.

This was a time when there was little care for the workmen. There were numerous stories of someone watching his finger get cut off by a piece of machinery and then wrapping the stump in cloth torn from an old shirt and going back to work. The only medical item on the island was some iodine that the men had bought themselves. But despite the loss of fingers and probably some other body parts the chains were made. A lot of chains were needed because by the end of the war Canada had the third largest navy in the world.

In the winter, when the air was wet and heavy drops of moisture clung to the dust coming from the chimneys of the island's foundries, the result was smog. It was like the famous London fog, when everyone heated their homes with coal and you could get lost on your own street. London fog became a London landmark. But when coal went away, so did the fog, and suddenly the air was not poisonous.

On Granville Island in the 1940s, reports say the smog was so thick that workers would walk in a line, with each one holding the shoulder of the man in front of him, so that they would not fall in the water, which was not good for your health since it was as deadly as the air.

After the war the island slid downhill, becoming an industrial swamp. In 1973 I was working at the *Vancouver Sun* and was new in the city. I left the newsroom one day and walked around, wondering where the heck I had brought myself and my family. I wandered down to Granville Island, though I did not know it had a name. I walked over the short wooden bridge joining the island to the rest of the world. Because I was young, I stepped up on the edge of the bridge on a four-by-four-inch beam and did some easy balancing.

I was wearing my new brown corduroy suit, very stylish in the 1970s. The weather had been rainy, and the beam was wet. I slipped and fell, not on the road side of the bridge but straight down twenty feet, toward the muck. On the way down I thought I would die. I hit the oozing mud flat on my back. I was lucky there were no rocks in that particular spot. But now I was stretched out looking like I was making a snow angel, except that I was sinking in the muck in my new suit.

"Help," I said.

No one heard me.

I tried to stand up, but it was muck right down to the centre of the earth. My feet found nothing to hold onto. I fell on my knees in my new suit, and then tilted forward, sticking out my arms and hands, which also sank in the mud.

"Help."

A fellow wearing a welding hat looked over the side.

"What are you doing down there?"

"I fell."

"Are you hurt?"

"No, just stuck."

He left without saying a word and returned with a ladder. He leaned it against the side of the bridge and walked away, sort of a throwback to the days when you cut off a finger and just kept going. Granville Island was my kind of place.

I climbed up, and there was no one there. No one to say, "You are as dumb as dog poop." Or, "What the heck were you doing down there in the muck? It's bad for your suit."

No one.

So I walked back to my car parked outside the *Sun* office on Granville Street and got in and drove home to the duplex my wife and I had rented and went into the shower with my suit still on.

"Neat place," I thought. "There must be a lot of characters here." So we stayed.

A few years after that, Granville Island was turned into a public market and became one of the most successful enterprises on the West Coast. You can buy fudge or quail or salmon or lox there. You are surrounded by flowers and jewellery and blown glass and art, lots of art.

And there are still two of the original industries operating: Ocean Concrete and a foundry that melts iron ingots into red-hot metal in blast furnaces. The metal is beaten and shaped into machine parts. It is incredible to watch; just look through their windows. The workers will wave to you.

And there is the Emily Carr Institute of Art & Design, which is famous around the world. And inside on display was a rotting plate full of steak and potatoes and vegetables. Artists are strange people.

The concrete company, which is next to the art school, now has in front of it a piece of art, a mobile with steel balls running up and down through seemingly endless paths and chutes and guide wires. If you watch it and follow the balls you learn how concrete is made. Educational art. The pair who made it, Cheryl Hamilton and Mike Vandermeer, have a studio called IE Creative Artwork on the island. They are making a living from art, and that alone is an art. They both went to Emily Carr.

"Do you understand the rotting food on display?" I asked.

"It's art," they said. "You don't have to understand it."

And art, like the island, like the food, like the history, like the smog, like the quail eggs and fresh bread and flowers and buskers and million-dollar yachts and mini ferry boats, has a life of its own. For a sandbar, it is one cool place.

Homeless Art

I was down at the fishermen's dock across from Granville Island. Now there's a cultural divide. On one side of the water, expensive yachts and sailboats. On the other side, fishing boats, which are tied up most of the year now because government regulations have cut back fishing to a few mini openings at best. Many of the fishing boats are for sale. It is not a good time to be a fisherman.

Fishing used to be British Columbia's number two industry. Logging was number one, but to be a logger you had to go into the woods and risk your life and work all day and get very little in return. While to be a fisherman, you only had to go out to sea and work all day and risk your life and get very little in return. You can see the advantage to fishing.

You did not need a licence or a permit to fish in the early days. All you needed was a small boat that you rowed out of Granville Island or out of Steveston. Depending on where you were, you put out a net and hung on or put out a line and a hook and hung on. That was at six in the morning because everyone started at six. Then you waited and worked while the rain poured over you. If there was a bad storm, you might have a little tent to crawl into, but if you did that you could not pull in your net and you lost fish. So you did not go into the shelter unless the weather was so bad you thought you would drown if you stayed out any longer. Then you crawled into the tent and hung on tight because you were in a tiny boat and the storm was tossing it up and down like a cork in a washing machine. You had no idea what a washing machine was, but you did know storms. There was no thought of returning to land because then you would make no money. Soon the storm would end, maybe, and you could go back to fishing.

At six at night, which you knew had come if you were fishing off Burrard Inlet because you could hear the Nine O'Clock Gun, which was fired at six back then, you headed home to the dock across from Granville Island. You unloaded your catch, and then the poor fellow who was taking the night shift climbed into the boat and rowed out to fish until six in the morning, when it would be your turn again.

Don't let anyone ever tell you that the ancestors of this place were anything less than supermen.

And so we come to today. The fishermen's dock across from Granville Island is peaceful because, basically, there are no more fish. The fishing factories from a dozen other nations are offshore with nets that spread halfway across the Pacific, and they are cleaning out the oceans of life. It is not a good time to be a fisherman, or a fish.

I have done stories about the cats that live on boats, and the gardens that are planted on boats, and the Christmas decorations that are strung across boats. But today I heard a guy with a knapsack on his back a few piers over shouting to me: "Hey, you want your boat painted?"

No, I think, I don't want my boat painted. I don't have a boat. And if I had a boat, I would not want someone who was walking around the docks painting it because I am sure it takes a skilled craftsman to know how to paint a boat. Furthermore, I didn't even know boats needed painting.

"Twenty dollars," he says. He is walking along the dock toward me now.

I can't pass up a bargain, even if I don't have a boat. That's pretty cheap. I figure it would cost a hundred dollars just to paint my bathroom, and my bathroom is smaller than a rowboat.

"Which one's yours?" asks the guy.

"I don't have a boat," I say.

"Well, then, why are you down here?"

This guy is rude and obnoxious and self-confident. I like him.

"I like looking at boats."

"I paint them," he says.

On his back I can see an easel.

"You mean paint as in paint?" I ask.

"Of course I mean paint."

"Paint? Like a picture?" I say.

He shakes his head at me. It is hard to deal with people who lack basic language skills, but he tries again.

"Yes, paint as in pictures."

"Would you paint that one?" I ask. I am pointing to a small red-and-white boat docked in front of a large black-and-white fishing boat. Behind them is the Granville Street Bridge and behind that are the condos of Beach Avenue.

"Anything you want for twenty dollars."

He removes his pack and undoes his easel and takes a wooden box out of his pack. It has watercolours and paper and brushes in it.

He is like a first-class professional artist who tapes a piece of thick art paper to the easel and then studies his subject. But instead of working in a studio full of supplies, this guy picks up an empty paper coffee cup, then leans over the dock and fills it with sea water. Into that he dips one of his brushes and begins to paint.

While he works we talk. He is homeless. He has been homeless for twenty-five years. He is from Vancouver, but he learned to draw while he was in prison in Florida. He was there for various offences, mostly involving drugs. Someone taught him to draw with a pencil. He said that is the only thing that kept him going for years while he was behind bars.

After he got out he wandered the country painting pictures, almost all watercolours.

"Why not oils?" I ask.

He looks at me like I am stupid.

"I'm homeless," he says. "Oils are heavy. Watercolours are light."

On the paper, the small red boat and the larger black one are coming to as much life as they have on the water. He paints fast and beautifully. He puts shimmering on the water and shadows on the condos. He slides his brush over the boats he is painting and leaves behind wires and ropes and nets and details and life, basically: the boats are becoming real. His brushes are moistened by the sea, and the sea is being born again on the paper. In less than half an hour he hands me the six-by-eight–inch paper. I give him a twenty-dollar bill.

It is an incredible painting. He could be making a great deal of money doing this on a commercial basis. His name is Peter Wallace. At least I think that's what he wrote at the bottom of his artwork.

"Have you ever owned a car?" I ask.

"No."

"Do you pay taxes?"

"Never."

"Do you sleep indoors?"

"When I meet someone nice."

He said he will not accept welfare.

"I don't want to rip off the government. I don't give them anything, and I don't ask for anything."

"Do you worry about the Canucks?"

"Are you crazy? Why should I?"

At that moment I knew he was more sane than most. He makes his way through life painting pictures of boats and houses and pets. All his belongings are in a knapsack.

After I did a story about him, a woman called me and said she was his great-aunt. She wanted to help him. She said his parents were ultrareligious and strict, and he had rebelled by leaving home and finding drugs. His sister had turned to prostitution. Too much of one thing often leads to too much of another.

I found him a few days later and gave him her phone number. He called. I believe they met, but then he went on his way again with his knapsack and his paintbrushes. I got several more calls from people who had bought his paintings years earlier. They wanted to know where they could find him. They wanted more artwork. But by then he had vanished, gone to another town or another country. His quest for freedom was his personal artwork, and art, whether you pay for it or make it, can both save you and cost you everything.

The Price of Being Born

It is not all fun. Life, that is. Just as all of you who have ever taken in a breath know, the pain comes hand-in-hand with the joy of living. Every birth will become a death. Every happy face will be wet with tears.

Death is what makes us wake up and say, God, how did this happen? But there is no answer. Death just happens and we try to get through it. Sometimes it is good to share the pain, sometimes you have to hold it alone. There is no right or wrong way. It just happens.

I got a call from a man one day.

"Do you remember doing a story about a boy named Conner? It was at Trout Lake, about a year ago."

"Yes, of course," I said with a smile.

I remembered it as one of those perfect stories that came out of nowhere. A boy and a girl were sitting on the smallest beach in Vancouver, just a patch of sand alongside a small lake just off Victoria Drive. It's a true inner-city park with its own mini getaway.

I intruded on their day and asked if they would tell me about themselves. They were happy, as anyone who is just falling in love is happy. They held hands and looked at each other even when they were talking to me.

Young love is the best, except for middle-aged love and old-age love.

126

Some chemistry changes in the body when you meet someone, and you glow. All the world becomes beautiful.

That was the story. Love on the beach, and afterwards I felt good. Can you imagine? They pay me to feel good. What a lucky day I had.

And then a year later came the phone call.

"Yes, I remember Conner."

"I'm sorry," said the man on the phone, "to tell you he died. He was killed in a car crash last night."

"I'm so sorry," I said.

"We were wondering," he asked, "if you could do another story about him."

When do the tears start, I wondered? Sometimes the shock is so bad they don't start right away, not while there is disbelief. They come later, when you refuse to believe what happened but you know it is true. When do the tears end? Not for a long, long time. But meanwhile you grab onto any hand you can, and say, please, make it not so.

Why did he want me to do a story? I knew, I didn't have to ask, but I said, "Are you sure you want that?"

"Yes. It would be a tribute. We need something."

We reran part of the story on Conner from a year earlier, on the beach, happy and full of life and promise. We followed that with the scene of today, where the flowers were piled up at a corner only one block from Trout Lake. He had been a passenger in the car, back seat. Alcohol and speed, the same thing the police almost always say.

What do you say? You say it is sad; you say you are sorry. And at least for one moment the family knew that others knew. For whatever immeasurably small relief that gave, I am thankful.

The news business can be brutal. Geoff Fisher, a young, happy guy running the microwave truck, the one with the tall mast that beams signals from far away back to the station so there can be live news, raised the mast one Sunday morning at a school near Crescent Beach.

There were wires overhead Geoff did not notice. John McCarron, the cameraman doing whatever story it was in the school, saw the lights flicker inside the building. Something inside him told him what had happened. He ran out and saw his friend dying or dead. It was hard to tell what was happening at that horrible moment.

McCarron could not step up to grab him because he and the others nearby knew they would also die if they did. Instead, he shot the scene. News cameramen around the world spend much of their professional lives looking into the face of death and recording it. It is what they are expected to do. If you don't do it, you lose your job or you get transferred inside, where you only have to see it on the raw pictures that the photographers send in. Please don't say they should not take those pictures. Most of us are too timid to look at them, but they must be shot because violent death is no less worthy of being recorded than joyous birth.

In this case, we did not show the pictures on TV. We protected our viewers like most news organizations do. My story on Geoff showed the national flag being lowered at the TV station instead and said, "It never flies higher in our memory than when it is halfway down. And we never salute a person higher than when we lower this piece of cloth for him."

A month after, John McCarron, who took the pictures of Geoff Fisher dying, got a knock on his door. It was a policeman. John's daughter, Christa, age nineteen, had been killed while driving up to Simon Fraser University. It was only by chance that John was somewhere else and was not sent to the accident.

In my eulogy, I said that though we can't talk about it in a way that makes sense, at least for a while, death makes us see things we did not see before. It clears the fashions and fads out of our minds. It removes what is mindless and small and leaves us with the essence of living, not lipstick and sneakers, but kindness and love. In the end, those are the only things that matter.

That is what we have to give to Christa, and to Conner, and to Geoff, and to everyone who dies: the memory that life has meaning, no matter how short it is.

They Don't Come Any Braver

Grant DePetti, age nineteen, was murdered. He was dragged to death underneath a car in Maple Ridge because he was brave enough to demand that someone do what was right. I heard the news on the radio in the morning, and like basically every person in the province, I felt pain in my stomach as well as my heart.

Driving to work, I heard talk shows analyzing and dissecting the horrid crime. Grant had stood in front of a car that turned out to be stolen and driven by some teenagers who would not pay for their gas. They knocked him over and dragged him underneath the car until he stopped screaming. Mostly callers were saying that $9.87 was not worth a life. Of course it was not. But Grant was brave, standing among the bravest people who ever walked the earth. At a critical moment, he did not back down. It was not worth a life, but in that moment he stood with the gods of old, who became the symbols of what we aspire to be.

Over one endless shot of blood and bone and pieces of clothing dragged along the road, a shot that went on for uncountable, unbearable minutes, I said:

They say don't be brave because it's not worth it. The scar on the road goes on and on. Painful, just looking at it. Don't ever be brave, they say, because it's foolish. They say he should have let the guys go. They say that a fistful of dollars is not worth this. Nothing is worth this.

And they are right. Nothing is worth losing everything. We know that. And because of that, often nothing is what we do.

We are wise, and stand back. In little ways, when we see something that is wrong and do nothing. And when we see brutality and corruption and do nothing. Because standing in the way is not worth it. It's not our concern.

But there are a few, precious few, who will say no. No, you can't get away with doing something wrong. No. I'm going to stand here and stop you.

So long as we have people like that, the rest of us will know what bravery is. They say no one's life is worth $9.87. No, it's not. But so long as there are people who stand up for what is right no matter what price tag it has, that life, no matter how short, is worth more than so many of us who live long.

The mark on the road goes on and on until it become unbearable. The pain is too much to look at, much less to imagine being under the car, screaming and screaming and screaming. The driver of the car said he heard it, but he kept going. And then it is over. The skid mark ends. So suddenly. Relief, at least for us. Over except for the justice, whatever that may be.

Justice is often absurd. In court it sounds like the perpetrator should be pitied for having a difficult life. But forget about that, if you can.

Think only that because someone stood up for what was right the justice in the court matters less. Doing what was right has already been done.

The Valentine Lady

Starting in March, Dorothy Walton collected paper doilies. And she collected magazines, which she hunted through for pictures of, well, of anything nice: roses, horses, dogs and cats, sunsets and sunrises, and hearts. Especially hearts.

By June her apartment in a highrise in the West End was filled with scraps of paper and doilies and pictures, especially pictures of hearts.

In September, she started to work. There was a lot of work she needed to do. Her husband complained that this was all Dorothy did, but he understood. He was living with a good woman, and you don't complain too much when you have a blessing like that. Over Christmas, her living room was filled with glue bottles and used-up markers and cut-up pieces of paper that would be cut into even smaller shapes, usually hearts.

By late January she was in a fury, not quite a panic, but the time was growing close and she had so much to do. She pasted red paper onto white paper, pasted a doily on top and then put a picture in the middle, often of a rose or a sunset. And around them all, hearts. By the time she was through, long after midnight in the second week of February, she had cut out thousands of hearts and turned them all into cards made of scrap paper.

On the back of each card she wrote a poem. There were many variations, but mostly they went like this:

Dear George (or Dear Millie or Dear Angela or even Dear Mike),
I will love you till Mount Everest rots,
Till leopards have stripes and zebras have spots,
Until nobody loses and everyone wins
And fishes weave cobwebs and spiders grow fins.
Happy Valentine's Day
From Your Secret Admirer.

And then she drew a heart at the bottom of the card. She put each card into an envelope and put a name on the front.

Dear Rick (or Dear Judy or Dear Mohammed or Dear Ruby),
I'll love you until there's no holes in Swiss cheese,
Till mosquitoes don't bite and ice cream doesn't freeze,
Until opera's performed by the cat and the fiddle
and Oreo cookies
have cheese in the middle!
Happy Valentine's Day
From Your Secret Admirer.

In the middle of the night on February 13, she would go around to every apartment in the highrise and quietly slide a card under the door. As the years went by she included other highrises. After years of that, and long after she retired, she continued to mail the cards out from Kamloops, where she had settled.

Before she left, she had taken the time and trouble to get everyone's name and address and apartment number. As usual, she collected the paper and the doilies and the pictures and wrote the cards and then she bought the stamps.

"Why?" I asked.

"Because it makes them feel good," she said. "So many of them are lonely.

So many have no one to hug. They get a card and feel like someone is out there loving them."

That was it. There had been no great crisis, at least none that I knew of, in her life. She just did it because she wanted to.

Eventually, it got to be too much. Her hands were tired, and collecting had become all-consuming. She had done it for twenty years. So she cut down on the cards—to just a few hundred.

Valentine was not the only saint.

Garbageman's Birthday

Roger Hope is freezing. It is seven thirty in the morning of Halloween, and frost is on the pumpkin faces carved and waiting in front of doorways.

"When are they coming? My feet are ice," he says.

"You can't rush a garbageman," I say. "They usually come between now and nine."

"Nine? That's an hour and a half. I'll die."

Why is Roger the cameraman waiting? Because in most neighbourhoods the garbagemen come and go with a lot of noise but no notice. They pick up your garbage and are gone before you can run outside with the bag you forgot. You leave a six-pack for them at Christmas, but beyond that you have no contact.

Unless your route takes you along my street. Then there is not only notice, but the garbagemen have become celebrities.

It started with one of the young mothers holding up her daughter to watch the garbage truck go by. Then the other mothers joined in. A toot from the horn of the garbage truck later turned into waves, then hellos, and eventually the truck stopped and there was a bit of conversation.

"Hello." "Fine, thanks," etcetera.

One of my neighbours, Barb, started putting up birthday messages in

134

her window. "Happy Birthday, Beth," for her friend across the street. "Happy Birthday, Caroline," for her other friend across the street. And then birthday messages for all the kids and husbands.

But that was still keeping it local, sort of inside the group. Then the neighbours started having driveway parties in the summer. On Friday nights I would come home and there would be four, five, sometimes six people sitting in a driveway drinking wine, the kids playing around them. Then came the chips and pizzas.

"Can I join you," I asked one night, "or is this a private party?"

"Do you have wine?" they asked. And so began my membership in the Whitman Avenue Garden Club. They all gardened, but the point of the club was to drink wine and discuss flowers, or maybe wine.

During one meeting of the garden club, after several bottles of wine, I heard my neighbours complaining about a problem down the street.

"That damn rabbit, whoops, sorry, the kids are still here, that darn rabbit is eating my flowers," said Beth.

My ears perked up. I am a reporter of what I deem to be socially significant events, and that includes rabbits eating flowers.

"I think we can catch it," said Caroline.

"What will we do with it after that?" asked Barb.

They did not know, so they had another glass of red.

The next day I asked for an early-morning cameraman.

"What are we doing?"

"Tracking some rabbit hunters."

"Who are the hunters?"

"My neighbours, and they probably won't like this."

The rabbit was owned by a nine-year-old girl down the street, but the family just wouldn't keep it in their own yard. To solve the problem three adult women were plotting to capture it and possibly turn it over to the pound, which was the only way they could think of to keep it out of their gardens. These three women would not hurt any living thing, but they did want to catch that rabbit. With the help of their kids, they constructed a rabbit trap on one of their front lawns. Jimmy, who was twelve, was stationed behind a window holding a string attached to a stick that was holding up a milk crate under which was a carrot.

"It will work," Jimmy said.

Kate and Alice, both four years old, kept saying, "There's the wabbit, ober there." Clearly the rabbit was way down the block because there went Beth, mother of Kate, running down the street with a butterfly net shouting, "I'll get you, you rotten flower thief."

"My mommy is good at catching wabbits," said Kate.

Isobel, the eleven-year-old daughter of Barb, told me, "I don't want to be any part of this." She watched with an eleven-year-old sophistication as her mother tried to head off the rabbit to scare it back toward Caroline, who was standing behind the trap waving her arms and shouting, "Send it this way."

Meanwhile, Caroline's daughter Alice was trying out the trap by pulling out the carrot.

"Alice," shouted Jimmy from his hideout behind the window. "Put the carrot back." But Alice started to eat it.

"Are you kidding?" said the cameraman.

But he took many pictures of the events that day, including one last shot of the rabbit scooting back into its own yard and hopping up the stairs to the back door.

"I guess we can't go there," said Beth. "But wait until tomorrow."

The rabbit never was caught, and the family eventually moved away, taking their rabbit with them and leaving the garden club with time to do something else less destructive like waiting for the garbagemen, who by now had become Kevin and David.

By the end of the first year of tooting and helloing, the women in the garden club were talking about Kevin and David like they were old friends.

"Kevin and David are coming tomorrow. Got to get the garbage out." Somehow, after many garbage-day visits around the cans, the women learned when the men had their birthdays. Kevin's was in the spring sometime, and David's was at Halloween. And now it was Halloween morning, icy and clear.

"I'm so cold," says Roger. It was now eight thirty, and we had been waiting an hour to hear someone yell "Surprise." It was impossible to say exactly what time they would come. Garbage collectors sometimes are slowed by, well, garbage. But the temperature was easy to tell. It was cold outside our shoes, and colder inside.

"Quick, look," I point. Beth is coming out still in her bathrobe with a winter coat over it.

"You could come inside and warm up," she says.

No, thanks. We are guys. We have to be ready to spring into action.

"You won't miss them," she says.

"No, thanks" I say.

"Silly," she says.

"Cold," Roger says.

Beth is carrying a tray with a cake in the shape of a garbage truck. The cake had been made the day before with Alice and Kate's help.

Caroline comes out wearing a coat and a winter hat. She has cookies. Barb comes out in a coat too, carrying yet another cake. This one has a plastic toy garbage can sticking out of the icing. The can had once belonged to Oscar from *Sesame Street*.

"Why are you all coming out now?"

"Because the truck is coming. You can hear it from inside."

Roger looks at me, slightly upset.

And there it is, turning a corner a block away. Roger spins his icy body and gets the shot he wants.

The truck is getting closer, and Roger is shooting. David is riding on the back, picking up the cans. Kevin is driving. As they stop on our street the three women and four kids approach the back of the truck, bearing cakes and cookies. You don't get this kind of excitement at political press conferences.

"Happy Birthday to you, happy birthday to you."

Have you ever seen anyone, anywhere in the world, even in Hollywood, where everything is made up, sing happy birthday to their garbageman?

Kevin shuts off the engine and comes around to the back. David is stammering and blushing.

"You guys are the best. Nobody does this," says David.

The women give both of the men hugs and the girls give them hugs and David puts his cakes and cookies into the truck and he and Kevin drive off waving to the Whitman Avenue Garden Club, which is singing "Happy Birthday."

Then the truck stops at the next house, and David picks up another garbage can.

"Funny, it's not so cold any more," says Roger.

Hockey as You've Never Seen It

The Chilliwack arena is one of those small-town hockey rinks where everyone knows everyone else. There are no box seats, and there's no padding on the boards where everyone sits.

It is cold inside and noisy and friendly and after a few minutes the atmosphere is so warm you could almost open your coat. You see old guys greeting each other and kids running for their favourite spots. At least half the fans are farmers. They work with their hands and arms and legs all day and come here evenings to watch kids playing hockey using their hands and arms and legs.

The people in the arena watch for Derek and Casey to come in. The two of them always arrive together, and they always leave together. Even though every game is sold out, there are always seats for Derek and Casey. If they get there a bit late and the stands are full, folks squeeze together a little tighter so they can sit down.

And the game begins.

"The puck's on the near boards. The other team's going for it. No, now the Chiefs have it."

Crashing and banging is heard even at the top row of the stands. Casey speaks just above the noise.

"He shoots. No, it's stopped. Now there's a faceoff in the Chiefs' zone."

Casey takes a sip of his pop. His throat has to last for the next hour.

"He shoots. He scores!"

Derek, Casey and five hundred other fans stand and scream and throw their arms up. Derek is still smiling when he sits, and both the play and the play-by-play resume.

Derek was born without eyes. He has a university degree. His best friend is Casey. His favourite sport is hockey. When the game is over and he picks up his white cane, he and Casey leave talking about the incredible save the goalie made with one second to go that let their team win. Derek's face is looking up toward where the scoreboard is. He doesn't know that. He doesn't care. He is seeing a replay of that great save.

The Chiefs are gone now. That doesn't matter. The game goes on, and as everyone who has ever played anything knows, winning is always possible if you have a good teammate.

A Beautiful Hog

I met Keith Johnson of Chilliwack long before the hockey game with Derek and Casey. Keith's interests were also loud and fast.

Keith loved Harleys. Keith was as much of a biker as you can be a biker without being an outlaw. He rode Harleys. He lived for Harleys. Then he got diabetes, and that evil disease came in like an eraser and rubbed the sight out of his eyes. He was in his forties.

He went through despair and hopelessness and of course thoughts of suicide. Who has ever gone through a life without thinking, in times of great pain, that not to be is the answer? But somewhere in Keith's blackness someone played some blues on a harmonica for him. It was magical, and Keith learned to do the same. He got so good at the blues that he bought ten harmonicas, each with a different octave. He wore them on a kind of bandolier slung over his shoulder and across his chest.

He could play the blues until it melted your soul. But he loved his Harleys. So one day he walked into the Chilliwack Harley Davidson showroom with his wife, tapping his white cane, and said, "I want to buy your best."

"Man, were they freaked out," he told me. "Here I am blind as a bat and buying a bike."

"He played with their minds," said his wife, Jackie.

And the minds of the salesmen were scrambled.

"Can we sell a bike to a blind guy?" asked one.

"Why not?" said the manager.

"Isn't it against the law or something?" asked the salesman.

"Let him sign for it, but don't let him drive it away."

They paused.

"How does he sign for it?"

In the end, Keith bought his new Harley and ran his hands over the smooth body. He fingered the engine and slid his touch up to the gears and then over the saddle.

"Perfect," he said. "We'll ride tonight."

To the relief of the sales staff, a friend of Keith's, who had driven motor-cycles during the war for the Canadian army, got out of his truck and onto the bike and turned the key. Keith climbed on the seat behind his friend. With a little twist of the wrist, the engine roared and they took off.

When I saw them, they were cruising down a country road. Keith had the biggest smile on earth on his face.

"I love the sound," he shouted to me as we drove alongside, shooting the scenes. "I love the wind. I love life," he yelled.

And then, in one of those moments that Hollywood writers spend hours cooking up and directors spend days trying to shoot, Keith pulled out one of his harmonicas and started playing something from Muddy Waters as he rode along on the back of his Harley.

We could hear it, we could see it, and that became the story. Blind? Not in his eyes. Bless you, Keith.

A Christmas Party

Y ou want to break your heart right before Christmas? Why not? It's an excellent time, after shopping and tinsel and lights and parties have you exhausted and swearing you will be ready earlier next year.

Take a break and drop in at the children's Christmas party at the Canadian National Institute for the Blind.

Stop outside the door and watch a kid feeling her way along the glass wall between the warm room inside and the rain falling outside. Then watch as she comes upon the Christmas tree, and recoils. This is nothing she knows, and it scares her.

Then go into the party and watch the kids listening to someone in the middle of the room saying, "Ho, ho, ho." Their mothers take them up to the "Ho ho" and put their hands on his beard and they are frightened.

The CNIB people know what they are doing though. The organization is run by a man who cannot see and employs others who cannot see. They were easing the children at the party into something that would be fun, even if some of them were frightened out of their skin.

Next to Santa was a woman playing a guitar and singing Christmas songs. I forget her name. I apologize for that because she brought the kids together as I watched. She was the spirit of Christmas. She sang so softly, and the children moved toward her. She knew they were there, even though she could not see them. She, like most of them, was born blind. She, like them, had once been terrified of beards and prickly trees. With love and with songs and with patience, she, like them, would grow up to love Christmas and sing the songs that sound so happy.

Go there, if you have the courage. Go at Christmas and burn into your heart the truth that we must be patient and loving and helpful. Otherwise, we will all be in the dark.

Christmas at Main and Hastings

I admit I only picked the drunks, not the drug addicts. I understand alcohol. I do not understand drugs. And I only picked the older folks because, well, let's be honest. The young ones at Main and Hastings complain and whine and moan and blame everyone except themselves. The older ones say they were the cause of their own problems.

And of the older ones I asked a simple question: "What was Christmas like when you were young?"

"We had presents and a fire in the fireplace and a big dinner."

His skin looked like an elephant's, and his hat was pushed back so far I wondered why he was wearing it.

"We didn't get much for presents, maybe a wooden car for me and a rag doll for my sister, but we didn't care. Our parents were there and it was warm and we were happy."

Then I asked a woman who hid her face in a scarf.

"We had the sweetest time. I loved Christmas. We lived on the Prairies, and it was cold, but it was warm inside our house and we had singing and happy times."

I did not ask people why they were there or what happened to them or what they were doing for Christmas now. Actually, to be truthful, I did ask one tough fellow what he would do that Christmas and he said he would get drunk.

"That's a shame," I said.

"I know," he answered, "but I had a good time as a kid. We played and spent the whole day running around the house and driving our parents nuts." He had a smile on his worn-out face. He was back, for at least a moment, running around his house and driving his parents nuts.

And then there was the guy with the black eye. There was no sense asking how he got that. A black eye at Main and Hastings is like a laptop at Burrard and Hastings.

"What was Christmas like when you were a kid?"

"I never wanted to grow up," he said. "I knew that was the best time of life."

Ten years later, I still remember the guy who said that, and the woman who hid her face and talked about singing. No matter what else we do, the kids won't forget.

A Very Tiny Christmas Story

Think of it from their side. Their office, their world, is slightly wider than their elbows and not long enough for them to take more than one step forward or back. They sometimes have a stool to rest on, but there is not enough room for their knees to stick out.

And there you are, staring at him or her with a scowl on your face because you have parked for just ten minutes over an hour and you are being charged for two hours and darn it, that's not fair. Of course, if he doesn't charge you for the extra hour he will be fired, and that will be worse than you feeling picked on.

The parking-booth attendant has that job because he cannot get work in an office where he can walk around and say hi to someone else. He is often new to this country, trying to learn the language and wondering if this is as good as it gets.

If he is working in an outdoor lot, he will freeze in the winter and sweat in the summer, and no matter what the season, he will get wet when you pull up during a rainstorm. You only have to open your window once. He does it all day. If he works in an underground lot, there is no rain, but also no sun, no fresh air, nothing except headlights coming at him, and scowling faces from those who have parked past the time they want to pay for.

You get the picture. It is not a job you plan on doing when someone asks you what you want to do when you grow up.

I was coming out of a lot downtown. I had been parked for ten minutes over the hour because I was trying to do my Christmas shopping and did not have a clue what to buy.

"Sorry, sir, but I have to charge you over the hour. But Merry Christmas."

His accent was South Asian. His skin was dark. His English was better than that of most rap singers. His sentiment was sincere.

As I gave him the money, I saw a little Christmas tree in his booth. And above that a tiny string of lights. No one was behind me, so I got out and looked around. He had a pint-sized plastic Santa standing next to his time clock.

His name was Ram Paul. He had been in Canada three months. This was his first job here. He was a Sikh.

"I see they do this here," he said, gesturing to the decorations, "so I want to do it."

When I looked through the front window of the booth, which I could not see from the car, there was a miniature manger scene, with Jesus and Mary and Joseph. He told me that most of the decorations had been bought by his replacement on the night shift, who would be coming in soon.

I called the office and luckily got a cameraman just in time to meet the changing of the guard. The man on the night shift was Malik Merchand, from somewhere in the Middle East. He was Muslim.

"I love Christmas very much," he said. His accent was different from Ram's. "When I came here I want to be part of this country, and this is my favourite part."

The booth was so small that the day shift had to step out before the night shift stepped in. They both wished us Merry Christmas.

It was almost like going to church. In fact, it *was* like going to church: same feeling.

Christmas in Reverse

"**W**rite something about Christmas. It's disappearing," she said. She's right, I thought. My friend put it out like she was ordering fish and chips in a diner. Just do it. Write something about Christmas.

The Christmas that I had grown up with, the biggest holiday of the year, was evaporating like water out of a fish tank. You don't see it going down until suddenly all the beauty is gone. The Christmas that shut down wars, at least for one night, was turning into a generic holiday.

Not only was Christ getting left out of Christmas, but Christmas itself was getting squeezed out.

Shopping had been a threat to the meaning of Christmas for years. But somehow, even with the piles of presents, the little ceramic manger scene was still surviving under the tree and sometimes a kid would say, "Let me put the baby Jesus in the cradle," and mother and child would sing "Silent Night."

And then papa would walk into the room with Scotch tape stuck to his fingers and wrapping paper sticking to his shoes and they would all sing. This actually happened, until the politically correct idiots started saying, "You can't say 'Merry Christmas.' Suppose someone who doesn't believe hears you."

And then they said, "No Christmas in the schools. We must defend the sensibilities of those who are not Christian."

And then they said, "No Christmas songs, unless they don't have the word 'Christmas' in them."

Then it was, "Just say 'Happy Holidays,' 'Happy Winterfest,' 'Happy Chilly Feet' and 'Happy Red Nose Month.'"

And by God, they were getting away with it. In a country founded on tolerance, we had become the willing victims of intolerance.

"So write something about it. Okay?"

Except what could I write that Matthew, Mark, Luke and John, not to mention Bing Crosby, Charles Dickens, and Irving Berlin, who was Jewish and who wrote "White Christmas," had not already thought of?

So I opened my notebook and drank a cup of hot chocolate and wrote what was plainly obvious:

Take a moment on a quiet street, with some old reliable things of life going by, no shopping, no panic. And think, what a beautiful time of year this could be. Sadly, as you know by just looking around you, Christmas is changing.

The schools have forbidden all mention of the reason for this day. This is in fear of offending those of different religions. In truth, it is only the politicians who fear this, not the people of the different religions.

But because that is happening in the schools, it also is happening in the homes. There is little talk of Bethlehem, and fewer mangers are being put out, and fewer and fewer songs are being sung about a silent night.

Also vanishing from our society, because it has been sidestepped inside the schools, is the word "Christmas." Instead, it is a "Happy Holiday." It is "The Best of the Season."

Forget the words: it is sometimes just a friendly competition of lights. And the purpose of this holiday, no longer an outgrowth of it but the reason for its existence, is becoming shopping. Shopping seven days a week. Shopping late at night, and shopping in a panic to satisfy the urge to possess things that are shown on television. Inside some homes there is great sadness, even depression, because some of those urges cannot fit into shredded budgets or cannot be found on the shelf because someone else got the very last road-rage video game.

A long time ago, when it began, the day was much easier to understand. Whether you saw it symbolically or actually, Christmas was simply the celebration of a birth, a chance to start over, to have a new beginning, a new star to follow. Even atheists look for new roads.

It is something you cannot buy or worry about or decorate. But it can be found so easily inside us, each of us, and it comes out—as a gift—whenever we say 'Merry Christmas.'"

There it was. Not literature, but the best I could say. But I couldn't just say it, for heaven's sake. This was TV. We needed pictures.

Karl Avesfelt, an editor who is tough as nails and may or may not believe in Christmas, asked a cameraman to shoot some nice scenes of a decorated street. It was two days before Christmas, so we needed the pictures the next day to run the story Christmas Eve. However the cameraman, we guessed, had stopped off at a party before doing his shooting. Normally he should be fired for that, but it was Christmas, a time for forgiveness, and besides, when we got the tape it was too late to ask someone else to shoot it.

What we got were pictures of Christmas lights that strayed from the straight and narrow and swayed right along with the man behind the camera.

"My God," Karl thundered. God gets a lot of calls around Christmas. "What the hell are we going to do? There's nothing here that is usable."

I shrugged. Without pictures you can't do anything. If there aren't any pictures, my general rule is to take a deep breath and let go of the disappointment. You can't use what you don't have. My words would die, another failed attempt to stop the draining away of Christmas, but really, what are you going to do? Christmas is a time of forgiveness, and we were not magicians.

"I can fix it," said Karl. He always says that when it looks as if there is no hope, kind of like it was on the first Christmas.

As I saw him looking at the tape of jumbled pictures, I was thinking of a church in Austria on Christmas Eve in 1818. The church's organ was broken. There would be no Christmas music. The sun was going down, the snow was falling and the townsfolk were preparing for midnight mass. It was unthinkable not to have music on Christmas Eve, but the unthinkable was going to happen.

Joseph Mohr, an assistant to the priest, had written a poem he called "Stiller Nach." He pulled it out of his desk drawer and ran with it over to his friend in the next village. He was exhausted when he got there. His friend, a schoolteacher named Franz Gruber, played the organ at his own church. Please, write some music to this poem, Mohr begged him.

Gruber did, and he and Mohr ran back to the church with the broken organ. With less than an hour to spare, they got the choir together. Mohr scribbled out the simple words as quickly as he could and handed out a few sheets to the choir members.

The townsfolk filled the church. They expected to hear the organ. Instead, out of the darkness came twenty voices singing in German, "Silent night, holy night," accompanied by two guitars played by Mohr and Gruber.

The song filled the church, and after the second time it was sung, the worshippers picked up the words. Later, much of the world joined in the singing. "Silent Night" sung without accompaniment is one of the most beautiful sounds on earth. It is the musical equivalent of the three wise men, a sidebar to an event that touched the world.

What was Karl doing in the edit room just an hour before the six o'clock news on Christmas Eve? He was playing with the tape. First he ran the only usable thirty seconds in slow motion to make them stretch over the words. No, wait, that piece of tape actually had no ending. The end of the shot was jumbled. It was useless. But Karl was running it not just in slow motion but backwards. And he added, very softly, the sound of bells. Then he handed me the microphone and said, "Read it, and do a good job. This is important."

That piece got more response than anything else in my time at Global Television. Because of public requests, it has been replayed every Christmas Eve for more than a decade. And no one has ever noticed, or if they have they have not complained, that in the final few seconds, when I am wishing you and everyone a Merry Christmas, a car is driving backwards down the snowy street and several people who are admiring the lights on a house are walking backwards past them.

Bless them.

God! It *is* true. Christmas is magical.

The Haunted House

I t is all true. It was amazing, at least to me, and so I did a story about it. My house.

Not really my house. We rented it for ten years, long after we should have left and bought a house, but we could not leave.

In 1973 we arrived in Vancouver, and there was a housing crisis. There is always a housing crisis in Vancouver. We lived in a tent in a campground in White Rock for a month, while I went to work as a reporter at the *Vancouver Sun* and my wife hunted for a place for us to live.

She saw the mountains of North Vancouver and said she wanted to live there. We had no idea that when you live in the mountains you cannot see the mountains. She found a place, a duplex near Lower Lonsdale. We had no money. We had spent it all getting to Vancouver. The duplex had one benefit. The rent was cheap.

Next door lived pot-smoking young men. We did not like our children listening to their music, which was extremely loud, and we did not like our kids breathing in their dope.

"Would you turn down your record player and open your windows?" I asked them.

They said they would consider those options. Then they closed the door, turned up the music and lit up another joint.

"I wish we could live somewhere else," my wife said.

At night, after dinner, we went for walks. We would walk up to Keith Road, which had some lovely old houses on it. One of them, on a corner, was huge and beautiful, hidden behind a high hedge and standing alone like a castle on an English moor. That's what I thought, even though I had no idea what an English moor looked like, or a castle.

Every time we passed this house on Keith Road my wife would say the same thing.

"I wish we could live in a house like that someday."

And then we went back to our dope-smelling duplex.

One afternoon in 1976 I came home to a notice that the landlord was selling the duplex and we had a month until we were evicted. This was terrible because no matter how bad the place was, it was a roof. We did not think of it as an opportunity, just a crisis.

I went to work the next day at BCTV and asked in the cramped old newsroom in the basement if anyone knew of a place for rent.

A long-haired cameraman poked his head up and said he had just gotten a job in England and was moving. We could have his place. The landlord, he said, would not object.

He gave me the address on a scrap of paper: 262 W. 13th Street, North Vancouver. It was not far from our duplex.

"I have no idea what it is," I said to my wife that evening. "There are a lot of apartment houses on those numbered streets." I was just hoping for something clean that didn't smell of dope.

After dinner we walked up Lonsdale to 13th Street and headed west. We followed the numbers along the street, and when we got to 262 my wife looked up in disbelief.

"That's the house," she said.

It was the house we always passed on Keith Road. We did not know then that Keith Road stops being Keith Road at that corner and becomes 13th Street. We went inside. The cameraman's wife said we would love it there, but we should know that the house was haunted.

Fine, we said. Who really believes in ghosts? We would have another roof over us and that we believed in. The landlord said okay. The rent was also low, about a week's salary a month.

The house was on half an acre of land, and in one corner of the yard there had been an old horse stable. The ground was very fertile there. Inside the house were back-to-back fireplaces, a double stairway, wooden columns holding up the second floor, a butler's pantry, a ballroom and heavy wooden beams in the ceiling. Out in the backyard there had been the servants' quarters, but that was gone by then. It was an early nineteenth-century work of art, built by a hardware store dealer for his new bride, Gertrude.

Everyone who visited us said they felt something. We figured that was the feeling of the dark wood that rose halfway up the walls in the dining room and ended in a shelf that went around the room and was supposed to hold the plates you wanted to display. The doors were solid oak with old-fashioned keyholes. The only damage was the lock on our bedroom door, which had been broken and never fixed.

Everyone asked if the place had a ghost. But that was just something you said when you went into an old house, we thought. And why so cheap? Well, the landlord said he just wanted someone who would care for it.

We lived there happily for ten years, and every month I delivered the rent cheque to Vladimir Galenchinko, who owned the house. He was an auto mechanic who worked for Dueck on Broadway. He had bought the house because he drove by it one day and felt sorry for it, he told me. It looked like it needed care, and he somehow felt that if he didn't buy it, the future of the house looked grim. He never moved into it. He almost never set foot in it. He just wanted to own it to save it from the terrible fate he feared would befall it if he did not buy it.

For the whole ten years, Mr. Galenchinko never raised our rent. I increased it myself when I felt guilty. Whenever I delivered the monthly cheque, this tall, bald Russian man would take it and offer me tea. His house, near City Hall in Vancouver, was much like our old house, with lots of polished, deep, rich wood, but his house had many Chinese vases and figurines.

Mr. Galenchinko's family were White Russians, the dissenters who opposed the Communist takeover of Russia in 1919. They fled to the east, and he was born in Shanghai. He spoke fluent Mandarin and was a friend of CBC cameraman Ted Wong. I listened to them chatting. I don't know why it is odd to hear a white person speaking Chinese, but not unusual to listen to a Chinese man or woman speaking English. We have such stereotyped minds.

Eventually we bought our own house, a cookie-cutter place with no character at all. I stood in front of Mr. Galenchinko's door and handed him our last rent cheque. I had not told him anything yet.

"You're moving," he said.

"How did you know?"

"I just knew."

He put an ad for the house in the classified pages of the *Vancouver Sun*.

I did not know that at the same time a couple walked by our house every day, and the woman would say, "I wish we could live in a house like that."

The couple were Gail McKenzie and Mike Johnson who operated the McNews magazine store on Lonsdale. I bought newspapers from them, though I did not know them. I only knew they had a small white dog named Sassy, which they got from the pound and who curled up on a stool by the cash register. They loved him like a child.

I did not know that they lived in an apartment that was being sold and they were being evicted. They needed a place in North Vancouver, so they hunted through the *North Shore News* looking for a place to live. They found nothing, and they had less than two weeks to go. On the last day that the ad for the big old house was in the *Sun*, a friend of Mike and Gail's died. They read his obituary in the *Sun*. Next to the obit was the ad for the house.

When I got home from work that day, I found Mike in my backyard throwing darts at a target I had hung on the old carriage house.

"We have to live here," he said.

Something told me he was right for the house, but I told him, "The landlord is sending other people to look at it this afternoon."

"Can you help us?" he said.

The other people arrived a few minutes later. I could tell they were not the type for that house. They did not look like ghost-loving people. I told them the wind blew through the loose windows and the roof leaked and the basement flooded and sometimes there were rats.

They left.

I told Mike that if he had cats (he did) there would be no rats. That the loose windows made it cool in summer, and if he put enough wood in the fireplaces, it was toasty in winter. The basement had flooded, but only once. And the roof did leak. Rain came through the overhang and watered the flowers.

Mike and Gail moved in. When she called BC Tel to have their phone number switched over, the operator said, "I know that house. I used to live there. Do you know it's haunted?"

A month later a customer walked into McNews and said, "I hear you moved into the old white house. I used to live there."

The customer was the nephew of Gertrude, the woman for whom the house had been built. When he was a kid he had slept in the servants' quarters behind the big house. He gave Gail and Mike some old pictures that showed Gertrude and her husband sitting in front of the house in a carriage drawn by a horse. Some pictures showed snow around the house; people always take pictures in the snow. He said Gertrude's husband had died just a few years after the house was built, and she lived there alone for more than fifty years. She was a nice, sweet lady who loved the house. That was all anyone knew about her.

Then he said he had brought them the last picture of Gertrude ever taken. He slid it out of a large envelope. First they saw the peaked roof of the house, then Gertrude sitting in the front yard in a large wicker chair. When the whole picture was out, Gail and Mike gasped. At Gertrude's feet was a dog curled up on the grass. It was small and white. The dog was an exact copy of Sassy who at that moment was curled up on the stool a few feet away behind the cash register and who later that day would be going home to that same house.

Of course, there are millions of dogs that look like that. This was a mutt that combined many breeds. So of course it was a coincidence. Of course.

Then the customer told Gail and Mike that one day when he was in the servants' quarters, he had had a sudden bad feeling about his aunt. He ran into the house calling for her. No answer. He raced up the stairs, shouting her name. Nothing. He tried the door to her bedroom. It was locked. She always locked it when she went to sleep. He pounded on the door. Silence. He kicked the door in, smashing the lock, and found his aunt dead on the bed. The heart of the sweet little old lady had given out.

The door lock was still broken when we moved in, and when we moved out and when Gail and Mike moved in and when they left.

It was still broken after Mr. Galenchinko died and the house was sold and beaten into splinters by a giant backhoe. The trees were cut down and the graves of at least two of my kids' hamsters and one small white dog that had slept at Gertrude's feet were covered over. There are now twenty-four townhouses on that land, and no one has said anything about ghosts.

From Russia with Love

I was in a bathroom, a Russian bathroom. I could not read the words that said whether it was the men's or the women's, but I swear it had a man's image on the door.

The bathroom smelled. This is not being bigoted or prejudiced or politically incorrect. Russian bathrooms in 1989 stunk. I met a woman in Siberia who told me they cleaned the bathrooms in the schools every week, if they could. The smell was something you got used to, if you were Russian.

Another Russian mother told me she had trained her daughter not to drink anything in the mornings so that she would not have to use the disgusting bathroom at school. These are the things you don't report when you are reporting on a student exchange program and the object is peace and understanding.

But all I was trying to do that particular day was go, and I was constipated. If you want to be a foreign correspondent, think of this: constipation is your biggest roadblock. Different food, different time zones and an impossible task: covering stories about people you don't understand in a language you don't understand. But after a week you can think of nothing but your bowels. You cannot think of writing something insightful when all your thoughts are taken up with please, let me go this morning, I must or I will explode.

Then I looked down and saw that there was a woman's shoe next to mine, at least as next to mine as you can get while sitting side-by-side in stalls.

"I speak English. I am sorry if I am in the wrong place," I said.

"I speak English also, and you are in the wrong place," replied the voice from the other side.

I recognized her voice. She was one of the mothers with the school group from Maple Ridge, Ruth Olde. We were in an airport waiting to go to yet another Godforsaken dusty coal-mining town in Kazakhstan. The town we were heading for was in the middle of a vast area of nothing. "Nothing" is the correct description. Look as far as possible one way from the centre of town, and there was nothing. Look the other way, and it was the same view. It was a different cultural horizon for the ten-year-old kids from Maple Ridge.

But right now the problem was with my bowels and with the wrong choice of a place to find relief.

"I'll wait until you leave," I said to the next stall. Actually, I did not want to leave. I was hoping something inside me would leave.

"No, it's all right, you go first," said the voice.

"But I may be a while."

"I'll wait."

This was the reality of a trip to Russia. The purpose of the experience was that children from Canada would meet children from several parts of the Soviet Union and peace and understanding would follow. The stories that we did said that despite some of the Canadian kids practising with hand-sized computer games during much of the visit, peace and understanding would follow.

And apparently it worked because soon after we got back to Canada the Berlin Wall came down and the Soviet Union dissolved and the missiles that had been ready to blow apart the part of the world where the US missiles were housed (missiles that were there to blow apart the part of the world where the Soviet missiles were housed) were dismantled. So obviously the Canadian kids had some influence.

"What do I need to go to Russia?" I asked several newspaper reporters who had been there. "Do I need phrasebooks? Do I need to know the

Communist Manifesto? Should I read the biographies of Karl Marx and Vladimir Lenin?"

"Yes, but condoms come first," they said. "Then Marlboros, then jeans. And they must be Levi's."

Russia then was a land where everyone illegally worshipped the West, and the West meant Marlboros, condoms and Levi's. It was a land where Levi's did not exist. It was a land where everyone smoked, and they wanted to smoke what was smoked in the West. And it was a land where the most readily available form of birth control was abortion. Hence the hunger for Levi's, Marlboros and condoms.

My wife saw me packing.

"That's a lot of blue jeans," she said.

"For others," I answered.

"I thought you gave up smoking," she continued.

"They're for others too," I said.

She gave me the wifely look that says, I doubt everything you say but I'll keep smiling. Then she continued.

"And those?" She didn't point so much as gesture toward the fifty packs of condoms.

"For others," I said.

"I assumed that, but what are you going to do with them?"

"Give them away."

Then came that wifely smile again.

"Honest," I said. "I'm giving them away."

"Why are you acting guilty?"

"I'm not. I'm just explaining."

I'm a guy, and my wife had seen me with condoms as I was going away on a trip. There are things in life that are not fair, and being a guy in that situation is one of them.

I had no trouble giving away the Levi's. I only took five pairs, more than my suitcase could hold, and they went to the first five nice people I met. The jeans were supposed to be bribes, but I got nothing in return for them.

The cigarettes went quickly too. It was not hard to give away a pack. The only problem was that after you did you had to have several other packs to give away to those who saw you giving away the first pack. So the cigarettes went fast. They were also supposed to be bribes, but I got nothing in return for them.

Mike Timbrell, the cameraman on the trip, traded his Marlboros for tomatoes in nearly every market we passed. The main food we were getting was boiled eggs and something he called blue meat. Tomatoes were the only thing he recognized. One pack of Marlboros would net him three or four tomatoes, so he got healthy while the traders, who were overjoyed with the deal, would eventually die from the tobacco they got. Funny how life works.

That left me with the condoms. Okay, I'm a prude. During the sexual revolution of the sixties and seventies I was working nights. I had a wife and two kids. "Don't you even think those thoughts," my wife had warned me, and I take her warnings seriously.

Not only was I well warned, but I had read lots of those spy stories where somebody starts with a little hanky-panky with a Russian agent and winds up in the Gulag. So, no.

I could have given the condoms to men, but I was seldom with men. Mostly, as in most countries, cultures and religions, it was women who did the organizing and event planning and inviting and caring and welcomed us when we got somewhere. Every time we were at an event, Russian women were in charge. Whenever I stayed at someone's apartment, it was with a woman, usually one with children. Usually the woman had the shape of a football player. I was not going to offer her a bunch of condoms. Either I would be slapped by someone who looked like a fullback or I would be thrown out.

With only two days of our trip left, I was dying from my plugged-up problem and still had enough condoms to start a brothel. The last place we stayed in was Karaganda, the most remote of all coal-mining towns on earth. Stalin sent his enemies to Siberia. He sent those he really did not like to Karaganda.

Mike and I were housed with a woman named Katarina. She was tough, squat, spoke some English and had been given a chicken by party officials to feed us. She was happy, but I was sad that it took us visiting to get her one chicken.

On our last night in her apartment she cornered me outside the kitchen and told me that her husband had gone away and never come back. She put her arms around me. She pressed forward. I pressed backwards. Mike was sleeping.

"No." I said. "I'm married."

She pressed closer.

It was like a Woody Allen movie, where everything that should go one way was heading another. I slipped into the bathroom and locked the door. This was not a time to relieve my other problem, which by now was an obsession, because to do that you have to be relaxed. With Katarina outside the door I was not relaxing. I waited for a while, and by the time I opened the door she was gone.

The next morning I left all my little packages of latex on the bed in Katarina's apartment.

Years later, during one of the many exchange programs that came out of that first visit, I heard that she had slipped illegally into the US. She eventually became successful, I heard. I hope she enjoyed what I left behind.

Now back to that other bathroom.

"All right. I have waited long enough," said the voice in the stall next door. "It is time for you to leave." The voice was firm. Ruth had three of her own kids along with her, and like the other two mothers on the trip, she was in charge of events, planning and wiping away tears. When she said I should leave first, there was no room for discussion. I left, and I carried my burden with me.

On our way home from Russia we stopped for a day in London. And there, in a hotel, while the kids were eating hamburgers, which they later said was the best part of the trip, and then touring Windsor Castle, I found relief. That is more than you need to know, unless you want to be a foreign correspondent.

Going Home

I was going back to New York for the first anniversary of 9/11. Don't believe those who say you can never go home again. You can. But you will visit only in your memory.

Before I left, I thought of all the things I wanted to do. I wanted to go fishing with Jimmy Lee. We used to sit on the street and lower strings with safety pins attached into the sewers, trying to hook rats. And I wanted to climb with a bunch of guys onto the factory roof and try to see Vanessa undressing through her bedroom window. But Vanessa is now a nun. And Jimmy Lee is dead.

So I wanted to walk across the Brooklyn Bridge as I had for years and watch the World Trade Center. On the bridge I would see the twin towers and think, "God, even to me, born here, they look so big." They were not so much buildings as attitude, like everything in New York.

Some think surviving in New York depends half on your attitude. Some say living there is all attitude. Wrong and wronger. You need attitude at time and a half just to get lunch in a deli. You put your nose two inches from someone else and say, "You talkin' to me?" But they have more attitude than you, and before you can blink they stare you down and say, "I said dis is my bowl of soup."

Attitude is knowing when to stand up, when to bend, when to face off in

164

the bottom of the ninth inning and give it all you have and suffer the consequences no matter what—and when to duck and say nothing. Attitude is in the guys in hard hats working six inches from unending traffic and knowing that drivers have too much respect for them to hit them. And it is the stockbrokers working out of telephone booths on Wall Street after the towers were killed.

Only the gap was there now, an ugly hole in Manhattan, like when teeth are kicked out in a fight. Spotlights burned through the night air where the Trade Center had stood, a temporary tombstone for nearly three thousand people who got a hammer in the back of the head and for two buildings that used to say, "I am, I am ahead of you, get behind me, but only if you are fast and smart and brave enough."

I wanted to walk by those buildings and feel at home. But they were like Jimmy Lee and Vanessa: they had gone to other worlds. They were not the way I remembered them. They were no longer as they'd been when I grew up and fell in love in their shadows and learned about people and crime and heroism. They were not there. There was only the hole, the gap, the emptiness, the hollow bitterness, and I was wondering, when I got to talk to those who were still New Yorkers: Would they be bitter? Would they want revenge? Would they still say, as they had right after the towers died, that they were going to hunt down the SOBs who killed their friends? I suspected the stomach juices would still be churning because the New Yorkers I grew up with did not back down from fights. They did not go gently to their graves.

There were a few other things I wanted to do while I was there. I wanted to stand under the elevated train and let the sound of steel wheels on steel tracks on steel girders rattle through me. It is the rhythms of our youth that we miss the most.

I wanted to see if New York was kinder and gentler, or if some of the old folks, as I had read, were studying kung fu and then kicking the piss out of punks who tried to take their money. Old folks have been New Yorkers longer than the young punks have, and you don't mess with old New Yorkers.

And then I wanted to go to the hole in the skyline. And cry.

What I saw when I went home again was people in a very New York way. Some were praying, some were digging out body parts, and some were selling hot dogs to the tourists who had come to see the digging and the flag-covered stretchers. But the irreverent gumption of the city, the brashness that has kept it going and become a character trait was right there in your face.

"Get your postcards of the attack," yelled a street hawker with a Middle Eastern accent.

Surrounding that gaping hole in the ground, which was the grave of thousands, were souvenirs of the unspeakable. There were pictures of Jesus floating above the emptiness, and collector plates of angels carrying firefighters to heaven, and coffee mugs bearing the photo of the plane hitting the second tower.

"What the hell are you doing?" I would have asked the seller, except I could not get past all the buyers to ask.

Then I realized that though it was ugly and tasteless and stomach-turning, it was also the spirit that had made the city.

"You are not going to get me down, no matter what you do. It may be only crumbs I have, but I'm going to sell them like a wedding cake."

You got to be tough to survive, and if you are, you will.

Crime

I don't do crime any more. Police stories were my way of life from the time I was a teenager and worked as a copy boy at the *Daily News* in New York until I got tired of it in Vancouver halfway through my career.

I grew up in police stations and at shootings and riding in the back seat of unmarked police cars going in for drug busts. It was a wonderful life, but after a while the police retired and there I was, still reporting. Their pension plan was better than mine.

There were many reasons I gave up crime, but basically you can have a bad taste in your mouth for just so long before it gets too bitter to swallow. So I changed to reporting on the good things in life and wondered why I didn't do that thirty years earlier.

But one day in 2002, while I was out with cameraman Dave McKay, he heard over the police radio that a corner store had been held up at 33rd and Fraser. We were at 32nd and Fraser.

"Okay, let's go see, but I don't want to do it if it's a real crime," I said.

It was a real crime. The police were handcuffing the bad guys when we turned the corner.

"All right, you do your job, but I don't want to report on it," I said to Dave. "We can send it in as a police incident, but I don't want to do the story."

The bad guys were lying on the sidewalk. One of them was screaming that the cops were treating them like criminals.

"Get me a lawyer," he yelled to a man who was standing nearby watching.

"Are you crazy?" said the man. "I was in that store when you tried to rob it. Get your own lawyer."

I started to think this might be good. Crime with criminals facing the public. I leaned over one of the guys on the ground with my microphone.

He said, "I know it was a stolen car, okay, but we didn't steal it."

"What did you do?" I asked.

"Nothing. This is not fair," he said. "We were just in the store when it got robbed by some other guys."

Then he added, "We were transporting the grow-op stuff to someone else."

"What grow-op stuff?" I asked.

"The stuff in the car," said the guy on the ground. "But it's not ours."

The back of the car and the trunk were filled with high-powered lights and troughs, which are used to grow tomatoes, if you like to have tomatoes year-round, or marijuana, which will make you a sizeable income but has no vitamin C.

"It's not ours," said the other guy.

By now a crowd had gathered around them.

They were South Asian and white and Chinese. They were the neighbourhood people.

"You better be happy that the cops are protecting you," someone said. "Or we would not be so nice."

"Get me a lawyer," said the guy on the ground next to me.

"I'm a reporter. You see the camera, right? You know you're being recorded. What were you doing in the store?"

"We didn't do nothing. We just went in to ask him for some spare money. We didn't rob him."

Sadly, the world is filled with idiots who try to rob a store, but say they did not, and who are in a stolen car, but say they did not steal it, and who have the equipment to grow marijuana in that car, but say it is not theirs.

"We didn't do nothing," said one of them again.

I could not resist doing a story on they who are so stupid. The reason I did it was that one of the cops who arrested the two guys said they would be out on the street by morning and working extra hard to make up for what they had lost. It is not just the crooks who are stupid. Our justice system does little to punish people who hurt others. It leaves them free to hurt some more and you scratch your head and say, this is stupid.

I moved to Vancouver because it was free of crime and New York was saturated with it. In the late sixties New York was suffering an epidemic of crack. It was dangerous to go out in the daytime. Old men who used to play dominoes and checkers on their front steps had gone into hiding indoors. Women, including my mother, were mugged, meaning they were hit, knocked over and robbed. Mugging is such a puffy word. The reality is so brutal.

We came to Vancouver, and there was no crime. There were no purse snatchings or muggings or smashed glass on the sidewalk from broken car windows. A pair of women could go anywhere they wanted any time of the day or night without fear.

Over the next generation, the scale tilted. Vancouver became dangerous. Drive-by shootings in Vancouver are common now. Guns are common, car theft is out of control, million-dollar homes are built just to be used as grow-ops, drug dealing is done openly on the street, and there is an epidemic of crack. Just like home.

Except that my old home had changed. When I left New York I was afraid to go into Times Square. There were too many drug dealers and pimps and hustlers and ugly-looking people who were waiting for you to blink so they could cut open your pocket, steal your wallet and push you in front of a bus. I was afraid to go into Grand Central Station. The entrances to it looked like Main and Hastings does now. And I, along with every person with an IQ above ten, knew better than to walk into the famous park behind the famous New York Public Library.

Now Times Square is as safe as Disneyland. Grand Central is polished and clean; the only thing a tourist has to be worried about is the bill in the oyster bar. And the famous park behind the famous library is now famous for outdoor concerts and quiet chess games and being a place to escape the rush of the streets.

What the heck happened?

Rudolph Giuliani was born the same year I was in the same part of the city. He did well. He had an advantage I did not. He is Italian; I am Irish. And I am not kidding.

Guiliani grew up in an era when organized crime was so big in New York that there were five major Mafia families, all running different areas of the city and different forms of business. The pizza industry was controlled by the Mafia; private sanitation companies and the cargo along the waterfront and at the airport were part of the network of organized crime. Plus there was the usual income from drugs and prostitution.

You get the idea. If money could be made from something, that thing was probably linked to the Mafia. There were tens of thousands of people connected with these crime families, from the godfathers down to the runners on the street, whose main job was to get coffee and sandwiches for those a little higher up. You got to start somewhere. *The Sopranos* was not fiction. These people all lived in neighbourhoods, just as other people in the city did, and they would take the bus or the subway or a cab to their crime headquarters or their criminal enterprises. They were just folks going to work like everyone else, except that their work was less than legal.

But there was one other major difference: the streets where these people lived were safe. If someone in the Mafia lived on your street, you had no crime to worry about. Usually they lived with their families, like most of us do, with uncles and cousins and grandmothers next door or down the street. And if something happened to Granny, literally all hell would break loose.

"My grandmother got her purse snatched," Three Fingers Louie would say. He would be in disbelief. He would be in tears. Three Fingers Louie, who had rubbed out half a dozen nonpaying loan sharks without a whimper of hesitation, would not believe that someone would hurt his sweet beloved grandmother. He would tell Snatch and Gimpy to teach that person a lesson. Three Fingers would spend the day stroking his grandmother's head while Snatch and Gimpy went on the hunt for some rotten, cowardly purse snatcher. When they caught him, or someone else, they wold do terrible things to him.

If they had got the right person, you would know for sure he would not be stealing any more purses on that street. In fact, even after his arms and legs healed, he probably would not be able to steal any purse anywhere. And if Snatch and Gimpy had got the wrong person, it would still serve as sufficient warning to the right person that repeating such an act would not be advisable.

In short, it was good to live in a Mafia neighbourhood, with the possible exception of when the members shot each other for misdeeds or the miscounting of receipts. Usually, though, they were bad shots.

Giuliani had grown up in just such a neighbourhood. He simply put what he had seen into practice on the right side of the law. He got the police to arrest the crooks and purse snatchers and drug dealers, and he got the judges to put them in jail and keep them there. It took a while, but New York is now the safest large city in North America. There have been many government studies and university theses written on what Guiliani did. Very simply, it was, don't mess with Granny and life will be fine.

Then in a gutsy move, Giuliani went after the Mafia. If you are going to get rid of crime you can't play favourites. The Mafia in New York is now stronger in movies and novels than in reality.

During one of my visits to New York I read a brief story in the paper that said the city had gone a week without one gunshot being fired. During that same period in Vancouver there had been six drive-by shootings, and two young men had been shot in fights on the street after the nightclubs closed.

A pity that those streets were not controlled by the Mafia.

The Ladder Thief

Don't mess with Luigi. He may be past eighty, but don't mess with him, you hear? Especially don't try to steal his friend's ladder.

What the heck does that mean?

It means that at the corner of Charles and Nanaimo, which used to be a vacant lot, John Horback sold his ladders. John was born January 3, 1912. I met him in 2002 when he was ninety. He was sitting in his car waiting for customers to come by. In the vacant lot he had four ladders set up. Each of them was a stepladder, each about six feet high, each made from kiln-dried hemlock. On each was a sign that said "Special." The price was marked down from $25 to $20.

"I make them so they will last forever," said John.

Most days he sold no ladders. Some weeks he sold one, because there were not too many people driving down Nanaimo Street who suddenly decided they needed a ladder and it would be a good thing to buy one from an old man in a vacant lot.

"I'm doing okay," said John. "It keeps me busy."

After he left his vacant lot in the afternoons, John went home and worked on another ladder, just in case he sold one. He would spend a week or so on each.

When he pulled open one of his ladders to show me, I saw that his left hand had only one finger on it, his ring finger, and that finger was twisted out of shape. He told me the others had been cut off in a mill accident, long before there was any such thing as compensation. He was simply fired because he could no longer do the job. So he became a barber because he could hold the scissors in his right hand. And after he retired, he started making ladders.

One day John left his ladders to go to the bathroom, something older men have to do quite a lot. He could not take his ladders with him or spend the time to lock them up, so he just left them on the lot. And when he did that, a young punk walking down the street grabbed one of John's ladders and started to carry it away.

But Luigi saw him. Luigi Prietie ran his own shoe repair shop right next to the vacant lot. He dropped the shoe he was working on and ran outside without grabbing so much as a hammer.

"Hey, you, put down that ladder."

The punk turned. He was sixty years younger than Luigi. He held a heavy wooden ladder.

"I said put down that ladder. It's not yours."

The punk started walking toward Luigi. Luigi tilted his head forward and started walking toward the punk.

Luigi was small, the kid was big, but Luigi kept going.

"You're not taking my friend's ladder," he said.

The kid took two more steps, then cursed and threw down the ladder and walked the other way.

"You could have gotten hurt," I said to Luigi.

"What you think, one kid's going to hurt me? Nonsense. I hurt that kid more than he going to hurt me."

He held up a fist made of fingers and a thumb and knuckles that had been holding hammers and awls before the punk kid's parents were born. If that fist had hit the kid or those fingers grabbed his neck, the kid would have felt pain.

John came back and learned what had happened. He was thankful to Luigi. The two of them had talked many times while they both waited for customers. The last picture we took was of them facing each other, talking and leaning against a ladder. John's left hand was resting on the same rung that Luigi's right hand was holding onto.

John is gone now. Luigi is gone. The shoe repair shop is gone. The ladders are gone. The vacant lot is gone, replaced by a row of nice-looking new stores. The only thing that's left you can see by closing your eyes: two battered old hands that earned their place in the world.

Ants in Your Asphalt

There are so many animal stories that are my favourites, but the truth is they are not really stories. A story must have a beginning, middle and end; otherwise, it is not officially a story. But when it comes to animals, who cares? They are still favourite stories.

Like the ants. This is another John McCarron story, done shortly after his daughter was killed in a car crash. He was going through another day of unbearable pain when I pulled up to his van on a road near Cloverdale and he suggested that we do something on ants.

"Ants?"

"Ants."

"Like ants on the ground?"

"So smart you are," he said.

He told me that while he was waiting for me, because I was late again, he had been looking down from the open window of his van and had seen ants.

"You want to put ants on television?" I asked.

"Just look. They're moving."

He knew that, outside of significant social meaning, moving is the first criterion for putting something on television. Watch a commercial—everything moves, otherwise they would never get your attention long enough to tell you their shampoo is better than all other shampoos on earth.

It was true. The ants were moving. He took pictures and I watched them through a magnifying glass and then we dropped some of his leftover granola bar on the ground and suddenly something was happening. The ants were grabbing pieces of the sugar-coated toasted oats and carrying them back to their home under the blacktop, over which thousands of cars were passing.

And they were not just carrying the oats. They were involved in a magnificent struggle to move pieces of something bigger and heavier than themselves. It was heroic, at least in the world of an ant. They were hauling crumbs up a hill, to the edge of the blacktop, and then to their homes, which would be like you lifting a full shopping cart by yourself up onto the roof of your house and then getting the contents down the chimney.

Suddenly, this was a story of determination and of overcoming odds. Can you imagine what those ants must have seen? Two giants larger than anything in *Gulliver's Travels* standing next to them, and cars bigger than Alberta thundering overhead, and they simply went on working, without any ant-sized concern. Pretty neat.

They got the crumbs packed away, and the story was over. It may not have been as good as going to Antarctica and watching penguins caring for their eggs, but on the other hand, why not? And the penguin story took tons of planning and money to produce. The ants were free and easy.

"How do you feel?" I asked John as he put his camera away.

"Crummy."

"Sorry. But thanks for telling me about the ants. How did you notice them?"

"I was just hanging my head, looking down and feeling bad," he said, "and they came along."

The Loot is Still There

In 1942 two men went into the Bank of Montreal at Main and Prior. It was a solid, squat building far from downtown. It had no guards at that time, and mainly women worked there, since most young men, good and bad, were in Europe getting shot at.

The two men who had not gone to Europe were nervous. They had done this before, but it must be terrifying to know that in the next few moments you will either get shot or get rich. They were banking that, because of the war, they would come out rich.

They pulled out their pistols and shouted, "This is a holdup."

They went to each of the teller's cages and pushed a pillowcase under the bars at the windows.

"Hurry up. Fill it or I'll shoot."

They ran out three minutes later with $40,000, fifteen years' salary for the average working man. They got into a car and raced away.

The men split the loot that night, and one of them took off and was never seen again. The other one picked up his girlfriend.

"Here," he said, handing her a $20 bill. "Go into the liquor store and buy us a couple of bottles."

She did as commanded. The man ripped open the top of one and took a long, burning drink. It felt good. He handed over the bottle, and she did the same. Then he did. Then she.

While they were drinking, the man drove into Stanley Park. They stopped somewhere near Brockton Oval, and they sat staring out at Coal Harbour. It was one of the few parts of the park that was still open during the war.

Now let's pause a moment. I would like to give that bank robber a history lesson.

"Did you know that an engineer in the Royal Navy discovered coal in the harbour you are looking at while you sit there with your bag of money? That was eighty-three years before you robbed the bank. And it was that coal that fuelled a lot of the money that came into the area, which went into the bank that you made your withdrawal from today. You owe that engineer some thanks. The engineer was a practical man but not very imaginative. He named the place Coal Harbour. Same place, same name as today."

"Stuff your lessons," would say the bank robber. "I'm a bank robber. I'm in a hurry."

"Wait," I would say. "It will look good on your parole report if you are trying to improve your mind. The name of the engineer was Francis Brockton."

But this truculent student wasn't listening. All he had on his mind was where to hide his loot. He couldn't go to the west side of the park. It was off limits because there was a gun battery where the Sequoia Grill is now. Deadman's Island was off limits too. It was a naval post, with a rifle-carrying sentry guarding the closed gate.

Dead Man's Island? Our bank robber knew the name, but nothing of the day in the 1880s when John Morton got in a small boat somewhere near where the Bayshore Hotel is now and rowed across Coal Harbour to this postage-stamp island. Morton got out and picked up a walking stick and began to explore.

He saw some old boxes tied to the branches of trees, and he poked his stick into one. The rotted wood broke, and out fell bones. He jumped back, nearly jumping out of his skin, then looked closer. Human bones. He opened a few other boxes. The same: more bones.

He learned from the aboriginal people who still lived in communities along the shoreline, across from where the Royal Vancouver Yacht Club is now, that almost a century earlier peaceful bands of aboriginals there had been attacked by some cutthroats from a different band from the Squamish area. When you're dealing with humans, whatever the race or the country, the story always seems to be the same: invade, kill, make peace, rebuild, invade, kill.

The cutthroat band captured some women from the peaceful village in what would later become the park. The men of the peaceful village offered themselves to the invaders in return for the lives of the women. The invaders accepted the deal, and somewhere near where Third Beach is now they killed nearly eighty of the men and left, having accomplished something in the grand scheme of invading and killing. The women, in deep grieving, buried their men in the traditional way, squeezing their bodies into cedar boxes and tying them in the trees so they would be closer to the great god in the sky.

Nice story, thought Morton, but instead of calling the place the Island of Bravery, or the Isle of Sacrifice, or the Rock of Love, he came up with a sensitive name: Dead Man's Island. The name became official.

John Morton had done very well since coming to Vancouver from Yorkshire with his friends, Samuel Brighouse and William Hailstone. They were looking for gold, but when they didn't find any, they bought a huge tract of land instead, in what later became the West End, but was just barren, heavily logged waste space miles from the not yet incorporated town of Granville and even farther from the busy Hastings Sawmill.

"You're an idiot. Why are you buying that? No one's ever going to live there. There's so much free land right next door on that giant spit that goes out into the harbour."

Everyone said that.

The newspapers called Morton and his friends the Three Greenhorns because they were obviously dumb as dirt. Why buy all that land way over there? It was more than an hour's walk from the centre of the new city at Hamilton and Hastings, where Lauchlan Hamilton, the new city surveyor, was laying out the streets. Not knowing what else to name the first street in the city, he named it after himself. And why buy that land after all the cedars had been logged? There was nothing of value there.

"No one is going to buy that land from you," the guys in the saloon said to Morton.

But Morton and his friends had a plan. They knew that to buy low and sell high, they would have to have a commodity that was both in demand and scarce. They took a calculated gamble that Vancouver would be growing quickly. They thought it should be called New Liverpool. It was a beautiful area with lots of opportunity. But then, how to make land scarce? That was easy: eliminate the thousand-acre tract right next to the land they had bought.

It took more than twenty years for the city actually to become a city, but by then Morton had gone to the city fathers and suggested that the big hunk of logged peninsula be turned into a park.

"What's a park?" said the city fathers.

"A place where people go to get away from it all."

The city fathers stood in the mud of the first streets and looked around. There was nothing all the way to the horizon but forest and clearings where once there had been forest.

"Get away from what?" they asked.

"Every great city needs a park," said Morton. "Even if we are now just a village of mud surrounded by trees, someday we will be a great city. What would people say if we didn't have a park?"

The unrecorded minutes of that meeting might have shown Morton and his friends giving a few gifts to the city fathers. I am not saying that did happen, just that gifts are always good to give, especially if the minutes of the meeting are not being recorded.

If anything was said, it might have been, "The gifts are for your children's education."

What did happen officially at that meeting was that Vancouver's first city council decided to petition the federal government to turn the peninsula into a recreation area. In short, to create Stanley Park.

"So that we can get away from it all," they probably said.

And naturally, property values right next to the park skyrocketed.

There's more to the story Mr. Bank Robber, so keep taking notes. Morton and his friends gave a big chunk of their land to the Canadian Pacific Railway in return for the CPR running a rail line through their land. Eventually they had trains arriving at one end of their property and a park at the other. The land they had bought for $1.01 an acre was selling for $500 an acre. The moral of the story? Instead of insulting people by calling them greenhorns, you should pay attention to what they're doing.

And think, Mr. Bigshot Crook. If you had gone into real estate instead of stick-ups, you might have lived a long, happy and prosperous life. Instead, you drove into the park and stopped somewhere near Dead Man's Island and, with your girlfriend, finished that first bottle. Then you opened the second, and after a while you staggered out of the car with a shovel and your bag of money. And somewhere in Brockton Oval, somewhere between Dead Man's Island and the Nine O'Clock Gun, somewhere away from the little community of squatters who lived in neat shacks with wooden plank sidewalks and tiny vegetable gardens along the edge of the park, somewhere you dug a hole and dropped the money in.

Then you finished the second bottle of whisky. Your girlfriend passed out. No kidding. So you drove out of the park with your unconscious gun moll on the seat next to you. You should have been ashamed of yourself, driving in that condition.

The next day, while you were suffering severe dehydration and your liver was gurgling like a stopped-up sewer and your head was splitting, the police caught up to you. Pity. There was a gunfight and you, Mr. Robber, got a lesson between your eyes.

All your girlfriend could remember was that you had buried the money somewhere around Brockton Oval, but she had been so blind drunk she could not remember where. No amount of coffee, begging, pleading, walking or resting brought back even an inkling of her memory. We now call that a blackout. So the police started digging. Everywhere. But they came up with nothing. Officially, in the police records, the money is still there.

I have another name for Brockton Oval: Home of the Stupid Robber.

Nine O'Clock Ashes

There must be a story in here that we haven't heard. There must be. The famous Nine O'Clock Gun is standing before us, caged like a fierce animal in a park that no longer has cages for animals, fierce or otherwise. The exception is the belugas in the aquarium, which get so much care and stimulation that I suspect they would find life in the ocean boring as well as deadly.

But we are talking about an old cannon, and I am talking to Dennis Dooley and Rick Harrison, gardening supervisors who know everything about Stanley Park. They both load the cannon now, and they both start laughing.

"What is it?"

"Can't tell you."

"Why?" I ask, begging, pleading, which is the way I get many stories.

"Because it's a secret," says Rick. "And if I tell you everyone will know."

Good point. But that is the point. A good story often starts with a secret.

What I know about the gun is that, even in the city's archives, it has a foggy history. There was no gun registry act in 1816 when it was made. The date was stamped on the side of the twelve-pound, muzzle-loading naval gun before it found a wet and scary home on one of countless warships that made Britain unconquerable.

The gun decks on those ships were squeezed tight. They were so low you lived your life stooped over. If you raised your head quickly, you would slam it into a hard beam of oak that you couldn't remember being there because you had your mind on something else, like someone trying to kill you with another twelve-pound cannon.

Everything in your world of the gun deck was painted red, below, above and around you, so that when a cannon ball from the angry cannon facing you came smashing through the hull and ripped open six bodies and tore off legs and arms from other men, you would not notice the blood splashing around. Of course you did see it, and you heard the screams later when the mangled arms and legs were sawed off by the surgeon, who was also the ship's carpenter, using his wood-cutting saw.

"Oh, shut up. Be a man and quit screaming."

The surgeon gave the sailors a shot of rum and a belt to bite on. After he finished sawing, the bleeding, raw stump was cauterized with hot tar. The severed arms and legs were shovelled off the deck into the ocean. The men packed in the underdecks groaning in pain with nothing to ease the suffering but their fingers gripping their useless stumps, were told to be quiet.

The Nine O'Clock Gun lived on one of those decks, facing the oceans with a cannon's fearless soul. In the late 1800s it was sent on a new mission, along with two other twelve-pound royal brothers at arms. They went to the new colony of British Columbia to defend against those colonizing Americans. Two of those guns stayed in Victoria and were later melted down and turned into bullets for use in World War II. The other one was given to the baby city of Vancouver, which was then not much more than a muddy land of sawmills and saloons.

How it ended up in the park is a guess. This is the way history is often made.

"What are we going to do with it?" asked a whiskered city father.

"I don't know. Let's put it in the new park," replied an alderman.

"Why?"

"Why? You want to know why?" the alderman said, searching for a reason. "Because there isn't anything else in the park except a hollow tree, and how long do you think people will be interested in that?"

The city father had no idea.

"I give it a year," said the alderman, "and then folks will ignore it. But a cannon, now that will keep folks coming back."

"And we could fire it at six o'clock to tell the fishermen when the day is over."

"We already have someone doing that job," said another city father.

That someone was the poor man who had the exciting job, at a few seconds to six every afternoon, of tying a stick of dynamite to the end of a fishing line, then lighting the fuse and as quick as he could, picking up the fishing rod and casting the line as far as he could over the water. With luck his cast was good, and the dynamite was safely far away when it exploded. This was one of the duties of the early custodians of the park. They could not simply throw the dynamite because they might not throw it far enough. A good fisherman could get it way out there, and everyone back then was a good fisherman, or else.

"So the cannon would replace that job? Isn't that taking modernization too far?"

And so the cannon was installed and fired every night at 6:00 p.m. The Nine O'Clock Gun started out life in Vancouver as the Six O'Clock Gun, and that is a fact. It continued firing at the dinner hour until the 1930s, when there were no more fishermen in the harbour. They now were far out in Georgia Strait and could hear nothing and the city administrators said, "Let us change the time to nine o'clock."

"Why?" said an alderman of the day.

"Because we've gotten a lot of complaints from women who say we are upsetting their dinner hour. The plates are rattling."

"But why nine?"

"Because seven is still too early, you numbskull, and eight is an oddball hour and ten is too late. So we will fire the gun at nine o'clock. Then the ship captains in the harbour will know it is nine o'clock."

"Don't the captains already know what time it is?"

"There's nothing like a good time check."

And so the fierce cannon continued as a timepiece. Imagine the indignity, the embarrassment that the old battle horse must have felt. What if a warship came into the harbour? What if other cannons saw it locked on land telling time?

But then in the seventies some kids gave the gun a thrilling moment. They waited for the powder to be set inside the barrel and then they threw handfuls of rocks down the gun's brass throat. Bang! The Nine O'Clock Gun fired buckshot at the floating gas stations in Coal Harbour. The mighty fire-breathing dragon of war was threatening again, even if it had been reduced to a peashooter.

After that, the UBC engineers stole the cannon. That was back in the days when the engineers performed amazing feats of vandalism and excited the whole city. Their most challenging adventure was hanging a Volkswagen under the Lions Gate Bridge. I still don't know how they did that. Another of their stunts was reconstructing a Volkswagen Beetle on top of the Birk's clock. I know how they did that, but I still don't believe it. With a crossbow they shot a line from the roof of the Bay over Georgia Street to the roof of the Birk's building. Then, in the middle of the night, the engineering students crawled across that line while carrying pieces of the car. My stomach gets sick just thinking of it. The traffic on Georgia Street ten storeys below, and a car door slung over your shoulder and your hands and feet holding onto a rope and you are doing this why? Because you are an engineer. The engineering students don't do those stunts anymore. Now they just go to classes and say that their courses are hard.

But it was the theft of the cannon by the incredible, amazing, idiot engineers that changed the look of the park.

"We can't allow that!" said the powers that be.

So a cage was built around the powerful twelve-pounder. No more the freedom of an iron-tough sailor, no more the excitement of looking out at nameless foes across the waves, no more the thrill of staring down the enemy. Now the gun lived in a prison cell.

But then came the day of the secret Rick and Dennis were talking about. The day Frank Getts, whose job it was to load and fire the cannon every day at 9:00 p.m., precisely, met a sad man. This was in the early 1980s.

Frank was drinking, as he often did, at the end of his day of tending the park and before his one-minute job at night. He was sitting on a bench drinking when a man sat down on the other end of the bench. The man was sad. His head was down.

"What's wrong?" asked Frank.

"My wife died, and I have to spread her ashes." He showed Frank the plastic urn from the crematorium.

"Sorry," said Frank.

The man's eyes were wet.

Frank handed him his bottle. "A toast to your wife."

The man took a swig. Then Frank took another, and the man took another, and in time life did not seem so harsh.

"I loved my wife. I always wanted to do grand things for her," the man said, and Frank understood. They were becoming mates, as only two guys sharing a bottle on a bench in a park on a late-autumn evening could become. For this moment, they were one in friendship, and friends help friends in times of need.

"My wife deserved the best."

An idea came to Frank. It was as though he were a nineteenth-century Royal Navy captain, and his mission was to win the battle of the broken heart.

"Would you like to give her a send off that she would never forget?"

The man nodded.

"Would you like a funeral that would go down in the books? But you can't talk about it because it would be the end of me."

The man tilted his dizzy head sideways.

"What do you mean?"

Frank pointed at the cannon.

"We couldn't."

"We could!"

The man relished the idea, but the impracticality of it, the crime, if indeed it was a crime.

"Can we do it?"

"We can," said Frank. "But we have to hurry."

Frank took the ashes from the man. What he was about to do was illegal. As much as you may think it is your God-given right to scatter your loved one's powdered remains in Stanley Park, you are wrong. No dumping in public places. And it is illegal to put any object—rocks, cannon balls or human ashes—into the Nine O'Clock Gun.

But Frank had a new friend, and the friend had a need, and besides, they had just about finished the bottle. Earlier, Frank had completed his nightly job of loading the two pounds of gunpowder into the cannon. On top of that, he now slid the ashes. The remains of the man's beloved nestled comfortably next to a mound of high explosives, kind of like their wedding night.

A few minutes later, when Mickey's big hand was on the twelve and his little hand on the nine, the timing mechanism twitched, and the gun blew out in defiance of law and in defence of a man's dreams. The woman's ashes shot out of the phallic symbol with excitement and pride. Her husband's smile cracked the sides of his cheeks. It was as good for him as it was for her. The cannon had done its duty.

Frank has since died, the widower has gone away, but the cannon that sent a woman into the next world still stands proud and firm. Go down and visit it some night at nine o'clock. When it roars, it speaks of eternity.

Liberty Ship

"**S**top, stop, stop. That's a Liberty ship."

Ken Timbrell hammers on the brake as though he is trying to save a little old lady crossing the street. But we are not on the street. We are on the waterfront, and the little old lady weighs ten thousand tons. And is rusting.

"What's a Liberty ship?" he asks in youthful, innocent stupidity.

"What's a Liberty ship?" I say in older, incredulous disbelief. "It's the reason you are here."

But how would he know? We forget everything, not just Ken, all of us. The Liberty ships saved his father, who had been a boy in England when Germany was dropping bombs on London. His father's parents were killed when a bomb hit their house, but their son survived and came to Canada and he became a news photographer and I worked with him for years. And then his elder son became a cameraman, and then his younger son became a cameraman and now was working with me. Then their father died. We are all connected, but sadly we seldom pass on enough stories about ourselves to our kids.

The Liberty ships, I told him, supplied England with bombs and butter and clothes and bullets throughout the war. If it were not for Liberty ships, Germany, quite possibly, could have won. Liberty ships were the number-one target of the U-boats.

There are other connections.

When I was in the US Air Force I was married and had two kids. You are not supposed to be married when you are a private and making miserably low wages. You are supposed to be living in a barracks and eating in the mess hall. But no, not me. I was married and living in a tiny shack off the base and trying to survive on one hundred dollars a month. Our rent was fifty dollars.

At night, after I had finished with my air force duties, which initially consisted of spraying DDT around the base, I worked in a restaurant for one dollar an hour. The pay was better than what I was getting while in uniform, and I could steal leftover buns and meat from the kitchen and bring them home after midnight and my wife and I would have a wonderful meal. And also to make some extra money I was trying to write freelance magazine articles. I wrote and wrote and then wrote some more and was rejected until my heart sank. I papered a wall with rejection notices.

Then one day I saw some ships in the harbour near the air base in northwest Florida. I asked and was told they were Liberty ships, and they were waiting to be cut up into scrap and sent to Japan.

"What's a Liberty ship?" I asked.

"Don't you know anything? Are you that young and stupid?" said an old sergeant on the base.

Liberty ships, he told me, had carried butter and bombs to England during the war. They kept England going before the US entered the war and then worked twice as hard after the US got involved.

More than 2,700 ships were built, so quickly that the hull was laid down and then the steel was swarmed over by mostly women driving in rivets and then the ship was launched three weeks later. Three hundred were built in Canada; they were called Victory ships. More than a quarter of all the Victory and Liberty ships were sunk by German subs.

The sergeant at my air base pointed to one of the ships in the harbour. "That one in the middle, that's the *George Ade*. It was built here during the war. My mother worked on it."

I learned that the *George Ade* had been torpedoed three weeks after it was launched. It limped back to port, knocked out in the first round of fighting. I wrote a story about the *George Ade*, named like all of the Liberty ships after fairly humble people. George Ade was a humorist from Indiana. The ship was built in Panama City, Florida, and twenty-five years later had been dragged back there to die.

A magazine bought the story and paid me twenty-five dollars. My wife and kids and I went out and got large hamburgers to celebrate.

And then came the day on the dock in Vancouver thirty years after my article in the magazine. "Stop. That's a Liberty ship."

We went on board, and I was twittering. It was the SS *Jeremiah O'Brian*, one of three Liberty ships that were still surviving. It had been restored by people who love history and had raised enough money to rebuild it and keep it going. It was returning from D-Day ceremonies in Normandy.

I was giddy. I was standing on the deck of a sister ship to the one I had seen in the harbour so many years earlier. I had not known then that the only defence the ships had was a single fifty-calibre machine gun on the bow. They shot at submarines if they surfaced. So the subs didn't surface. They stayed deep and fired death.

If the Liberty ships were attacked by air, there was no defence. The only thing the crew could do was coat the decks with tar so that machine gun fire from diving fighters would not ricochet. Service on a Liberty ship was not a way to avoid being killed.

But now I had the chance to do a story on the SS *Jeremiah O'Brian*, and if ever a story got heart and soul poured into it, that was the one. The ships were slow, squat tramp steamers, but I understood why some people fall in love with things that float on the sea. Now I was one of them.

A month later, when I was driving along Esplanade in North Vancouver, I saw a biker sitting on the seat of his Harley drawing a picture. It was clear once I stopped what he was doing. The stern of a Victory ship was hoisted up on steel poles. It was the beginning of what some hope will someday be a maritime museum over there. He was sketching the back of the ship.

Even though I knew, I stopped and asked him what he was doing.

"Drawing that ship."

A biker drawing pictures. That was odd. But who was I to question anyone who was large and sitting backwards on a hog with a sketch pad?

"Do you know anything about it?" he asked.
"It's a Victory ship, like a Liberty ship," I said.
"What's a Victory ship? What's a Liberty ship?"
So I told him.

Next Stop Chilliwack

"**Y**ou went how fast?"

I did not believe what he had just said. First of all, I did not believe they could go that fast. Secondly, he looked so dignified in his old uniform that I did not believe he would have gone that fast even if he could.

"We pushed her up to seventy miles per hour."

That is just over one hundred and ten kilometres an hour.

"In these things?"

I was looking at an old streetcar with a designed image of slow but steady. Don Bellamy was telling me that they were really fast and fantastic.

"One time I had a cop chasing me with his siren going. But after a couple of miles, he gave up. We were out in the Valley, and I guess he just went back and filed a report about how irresponsible we were," said Don.

Don was a retired city councillor. Before that he had been a cop. And before that a motorman, on the fabulous, romantic Interurban Line. The speed-demon trip he was talking about was the run from Vancouver to Chilliwack, done in an hour and a half. You cannot get on a city bus and get to Chilliwack now. A car is the preferred way of doing it, and if you try it at rush hour, it will take you longer than it did in the old rail car that Don was driving.

What a history Vancouver has. Streetcars could get you to anywhere from anywhere at very little cost in a minimum of time. Now the cost is high and the time is higher.

"We could still beat any bus or car," said Don as he pushed the throttle along False Creek, on the only track left. The Interurban Line had been rebuilt as a tourist attraction before it was ripped up for construction of the Olympic village between Science World and Granville Island. I hope it will be put back.

Don pulled the bell and said, "We used to scare the pants off drivers who did stupid things like scoot in front of us."

I had known almost nothing about this wonderful history until Ron Tupper, an editor at Global, told me that he had found a dusty piece of film in the bottom of an old box.

Ron is a neat guy who wears Irish soccer-league shirts to work and lives in sandals. I don't think he has a pair of closed-up shoes or long pants. Shorts all winter. What do I care? He is a magician with pictures, and he had found some fading beauties. They had been shot by a couple of motormen on the Interurban in 1950, when the future of the line was doomed. Busses had come into style by then. Those who sold rubber tires and concrete for roads were gaining political power, and the age of the streetcar was finished.

But the pictures that Ron found were marvellous. Two motormen had taken an 8 mm camera on board and shot footage of the world they saw through the windshields of several trolleys as they moved around the city. You could see Metrotown when it was still a country stop with grass and trees, and school kids racing down the tracks trying to catch the train. You could see deer running ahead of the car in Burnaby. And you could see the hundreds of men and women swarming to get a streetcar home at Carrall and Hastings.

These pictures taken at Carrall and Hastings were the most amazing because the building on the southwest corner of that intersection was Vancouver's Grand Central Station. You changed trains at Carrall and Hastings. You met your friends at Carrall and Hastings. You joined the crowds coming and going at Carrall and Hastings.

Once you were down there, you walked along East Hastings, stopping to buy a necktie or a dress or some shoes. Or you met your sweetheart for lunch or for dinner and then took in a movie or a live show. At Christmastime you brought your kids down to look at the window displays at Woodwards. What a wonderful neighbourhood, you thought, and what a beautiful time to be alive. When you'd finished looking, you walked back to Carrall and Hastings, buying a newspaper on the way and donuts for your kids to eat on the ride home. All the while, the streetcars of the Interurban rolled in and out of the building with the giant vaulted doors.

The vaulted doors are still there on one side of the building. But outside now are drug dealers. The streetcars and the commuters are gone. One by one, the stores along Hastings that sold donuts and lunches and ties and dresses closed up. There were no customers. Woodwards died. The theatres shut down. Even the newspapers were gone. Drug dealers don't have time for reading.

What happened? A combination of things, but the first was that those in command of the city wanted to modernize. Everyone always wants to modernize, and streetcars were old-fashioned. It would be better to have busses, they said.

In the film that Ron found are pictures of the last of the streetcars being unloaded from flatbed trucks under the Burrard Street Bridge, then soaked in gasoline and set on fire. It is heartbreaking to watch. You want to shout at the screen, "Don't! You have no idea how good you have it."

Once the streetcars were gone, there was no need for a terminal at Carrall and Hastings. Those who ran BC Hydro, which ran the busses, built a new modern headquarters on Burrard Street and closed up the old building with the arched entrances.

What you see on East Hastings now began when they shut down that building. In the crowds of tax-paying commuters there was no room for drug dealers. There was also poverty and the closing of Riverview and the rise of gangs that make much money from selling drugs, which all factored into the decline of East Hastings. But like dominoes, it started with the end of the streetcars.

Another thing I learned from that old film: there are still streetcar tracks running above ground along Arbutus Street. They cross Broadway and go south on their own unused right-of-way. Down in the neighbourhoods of

South Vancouver the residents have planted gardens alongside the tracks. Some are beautiful with flowers; others are little vegetable farms.

In the 1930s an Interurban streetcar would take you past where those gardens are now, and it would take you across the Fraser River at Mitchell Island. Part of one streetcar bridge is still there. Workers on the island sit on it in the summer and eat their lunch. You could get off the streetcar at Sea Island, which of course is where the tiny Vancouver airport operated. Vancouver to the airport, direct; no need to change trains.

When we entered this present century there came the need for a rail route to the airport. Committees of government bureaucrats and planners spent endless hours and bottomless budgets studying the best way to get there. They concluded that digging a tunnel under Cambie Street was the way to go. It will cost more money than anyone will ever be able to count. The construction has shut down Cambie Street for years.

There is no arguing that the end of the tunnel will be closer to downtown than the old Arbutus tracks are. There is no arguing that the old Arbutus tracks belong to the Canadian National Railway. And there is no arguing that those who live along the tracks on Arbutus Street would much prefer to keep their gardens than to see the tracks being used by commuters going to the airport. But the truth remains, the tracks are there. No tunnel needed to be built. It is not that much farther to get downtown from Arbutus than from Cambie.

But then underground was probably the modern way to go.

Rags to Faint

Success is the goal, I know. But it always makes my head spin to see someone doing well. Wait a minute, I say, I could have done the same thing. I am happy for the person who is successful, but I wonder, why did I step off the train just before it pulled into the station with the brass band and the prizes?

What am I talking about? I am talking in general terms about not buying an apartment in Yaletown when it was still an industrial wasteland, or one in Whistler when the only thing people did there was ski, not spend their days in boutiques and their nights in clubs.

And I am talking about taking pictures. I can take nice pictures of mountains and trees, so why didn't I do what Grant Faint did? I ask you. I asked him. He shrugged.

I worked with Grant in the 1970s when he was just out of his teens. He was a cameraman famous for taking incredibly good pictures and for a short temper. When he got bored with a reporter standing in front of him interviewing someone, when he knew that all the questions had been asked, he simply unplugged the microphone cable and walked away and started taking pictures of something else. The reporter would be left holding the talking stick and asking questions even though there was no cameraman to record it. Many reporters learned to be brief by working with Grant.

And heaven help you if you told him to take a certain picture. Grant would hand you the camera and walk away. Whoops. Wait. I didn't mean to tell you what to do.

The bottom line: Don't mess with him. He was a poor kid from the east side of Vancouver. One Christmas there was no food in his family's refrigerator, he remembers. A Christian group came in and filled it up. He learned to stand up for himself, and when it came to working together, he took the pictures, you took care of the words.

But while you were working with Grant he would stop at some point during most any story, take out his still camera and shoot scenery. Mostly it was the North Shore mountains, but also trees and seashores and birds and flowers, ordinary stuff. Then he would bundle up his slides and send them to the Image Bank, a photo agency in New York that sold pictures to magazines and advertising agencies. Grant had a dream of seeing his pictures someday in a magazine.

But picture after picture that Grant sent got rejected. So he took more and sent those, ordinary things seen in an unordinary way. And then one day while we were out working he stopped his van outside the Hotel Vancouver and told me to follow him. He went into the gift shop, picked up a nationally circulating glossy magazine, opened to a page with a cigarette ad and said, "That's mine."

I was looking at a picture of the North Shore mountains behind whatever cigarette was being smoked.

Grant's dream that he could do this was becoming a reality. The dream that he could take pictures of something besides press conferences and car wrecks and reporters conducting lengthy interviews while he held a camera on his shoulder and thought, "A five-year-old could ask better questions."

He took and sent in more pictures. Most of them were still rejected. But a few were bought, and that fed the dream. The year after Expo he quit the TV station and went full time into freelance photography. He had no income outside of his pictures. He had no contract. He had nothing but a camera and a good deal of East Vancouver gumption.

Jump ahead twenty years. Grant now has more pictures with Getty Images, which bought the Image Bank, than basically any photographer in the world. The company makes millions a year from his photos. He gets a significant portion of that. In short, he kept polishing his dream until it had a golden shine.

He works about four months a year, travelling to whatever countries he has an urge to see. He usually takes one of his kids and whatever friend the kid wants to bring along. His children have seen much of the world, from jungles to mountaintops to big cities and small towns. He takes 85,000 pictures a year.

Recently he spent a week in London, during which he shot 6,000 pictures. He cut those down to 500. The editors at Getty trimmed the pile down to six. Included in those half-dozen pictures is one of a Muslim family looking through the gate at Buckingham Palace. There is a man, a woman and a child. All their clothing is black except for the white cap on the man's head. The woman's head is turned back toward the camera, but Grant said she was not looking at him. She is wearing a burka, and only her eyes are showing. The child is standing between the mother and the father.

It seems to be a lovely black-and-white photo, but it is not. In the distance, smack in the centre of the photo, above the child's head and between his parents' bodies, is a tiny dot of red, a uniformed palace guard. In an eight-by-ten photo, the palace guard is about the size of the fingernail on your pinky.

The picture was not doctored. It is the work of someone who keeps working to get pictures like that. And that is where the story might have ended: another poor kid turning into a wealthy man, success based on hard work, dedication and drive. That's nice. He is a person to look up to.

But this story doesn't end there. Grant started going to Africa to photograph beautiful scenes in the deserts and jungles, and along the way he saw many children orphaned by the killer AIDS. He saw more and more children living on their own, twelve-year-olds trying to be the head of a family and young girls forced into unbearable lives because there was no other way.

He basically created his own charity, which is called Images for Orphans. Look it up on the Internet: www.grantfaint.com. Buy an incredible photo from a master cameraman, and all of the money, literally all of the money, goes to help the orphans. He has also made two films that have raised more money for the orphans. He has donated a large amount of his own money.

"I have been very lucky," he said. "It is time to give back."

Luck had nothing to do with it.

The Joke That Cuts

We all think we are comics.

I was in a drapery store on Kingsway in Burnaby interviewing the owner. The story was about some problem he was having in business.

After the interview, the owner's father came out of the back of the store to meet us. He was short, round of stomach and bald. His glasses were tilted forward on his nose, his sleeves were rolled up and his collar was open. He didn't have to open his mouth to be the image of a Montreal or New York Jew who has spent his life in the cloth trade. When he said hello his words came from the streets of the garment centre on the lower East Side.

He smiled, he joked about the weather and business, and his accent rolled out like a Yiddish melody. It made me homesick. I am from a neighbourhood where Yiddish and bagels and lox used to predominate. Now curry and jerk chicken and accents that would have been strange to my ears as a kid fill those same streets. Streets are like gardens; they change.

But in this drapery store on Kingsway I asked the old fellow if he was from New York. He was, he said, from Delancy Street in lower Manhattan, where he went to work when times were bad in Montreal, where he was born. For a while he was from Miami, where Jews from Delancy Street go when they make enough money to get there. Now he was from Vancouver, where he had come to live and help his son in his business.

He was like Tevye in *Fiddler on the Roof*: laughing, thinking, working, accepting.

As the cameraman and I were packing up to leave, a woman customer came into the store and began talking to the father. She was comfortable. She had obviously been there before.

"How much can I Jew you down for?" she asked. Her voice was loud and self-assured, and she emphasized the noun that had become a verb.

"How much would you like to pay?" His answer was subdued.

"Ten per cent off," she said with a mock Yiddish accent, "unless I can Jew you down for more."

"We'll see what we can do," he said.

"Give me a break," she added. "You know you can't help stealing from me."

I listened. It was not my store. A word from me would have started an argument: "Who do you think you are, telling me what to say?"

Besides, she was not intentionally being anti-Semitic. She was not intentionally being hateful. She was laughing. She was being friendly. She thought she was being funny.

The father smiled and excused himself from her and walked across to the other side of the store to say good-bye to us.

We shook hands, then he looked back at her.

"You know," he said to me, "I was born Jewish sixty-five years ago. All my life I've listened to this." As he spoke, his heavy accent no longer sounded lyrical. "All I can do is smile, and pretend it doesn't hurt."

Please don't say he should have stood up for his rights, that he should have told her off, that he should have informed her what she was doing was not nice. If he had, she would most likely have been embarrassed. Humans don't take instruction well. She would have been insulted and walked out and told her friends that the Jew in that store can't even take a joke. And the little seed would grow.

In British Columbia we don't make many jokes about Jews, mainly because, who's a Jew? "Are you really Jewish? I didn't know that. You don't sound like a Jew."

But there are the Chinese, and the South Asians, and there are the attempts at jokes by others who try to sound Chinese or South Asian or aboriginal, and you laugh—unless you are shopping in the next aisle and that is the way you speak. It is hard to smile when they are laughing at you.

To Walk a Dog

They are jailed in long rows of cages, barking. You walk by and want to take them all home. I could do a story a day in the city pound and never run out of subjects or an audience. Except I would be fired.

"Enough dogs already. Go out and find something else," says the six o'clock producer.

"Horses?" I say.

"No, you did horses last week."

"So," I say to Bob Cristofoli, who works at the pound, "do you have anything besides dogs?"

"Ducks," he says. "Someone abandoned three ducks on Victoria Drive. We found them waddling down the street."

Thank you, Bob; thank you, story god; thank you, rotten person who abandoned the ducks, which meant I could now do a story about them. But, really, you should rot in hell. I mean, what do you think you are doing dropping off three ducks on a busy street and then taking off? We should drop you off in Afghanistan without a phrase book or a passport.

Anyway, the ducks were neat because not only did we get pictures of them swimming around in a child's wading pool, next to some dogs that were drooling through a fence, but they were adopted in the very hour that we were there. They went off to a hobby farm in Langley, so I had a story to tell about orphaned ducks that were no longer orphaned. Talk about being a lucky duck.

The next time I was at the pound, I asked Bob again, "What do you have?"

At many pounds, including the one in Vancouver, you can volunteer to walk the dogs. It is good people who do this. Shelley Moore, a news camerawoman for one of the other TV stations, does it. I saw her one day near the pound with a four-legged misfit on a leash that was pulling her around the sidewalk. The last time I'd seen her was at a fire, where she was filming screaming people and heroic firefighters. The time before that she was at a shooting, trying to get past police lines.

"You do this?" I asked, being pretty sure of the answer.

"They need someone," she said. "And I have a few spare minutes sometimes."

When she takes a picture you know there is empathy inside the frame.

The next time I was at the pound, Bob and I were standing there talking when a biker came in. He had a shaggy beard, uncombed long hair, a black leather jacket, a beer belly, crumpled pants and big boots. My immediate thought was that he wanted to take home a large dog to guard his grow-op. But then I am a bigot, and the thoughts of bigots should always be discounted.

Bob greeted him like a cousin. "This is Glen," he said to me.

He handed the visitor a leash with a smile. Obviously I was missing something.

"You ought to do a story about him," said Bob, as the biker walked through the door to the hallway of cages. "He comes three times a week and takes out the dog no one else wants."

I ran after him. The biker was outside the cage of a dog that looked like a pit bull crossed with a Rottweiler and several other unidentifiable breeds of muscle.

"No one wants to take him out," said the biker.

He opened the cage, said some gentle words, and snapped on the dog's leash. Then he walked out of the pound and across the street to the park. I followed. After a few minutes of the dog walking and bladder-emptying and leg-stretching, the biker squatted down next to the tough-looking creature and started singing. From his lips came beautiful, melodic Irish lullabies. He looked into the dog's face and sang of the emerald grass of the old island.

"Why?" I asked.

He looked up. When a guy like that looks up, you remember the face: lots of hair, little skin and a missing tooth.

"My granny sang them to me," he said. "They make me feel good."

The pit bull crossed with other things was wagging its tail.

I backed off. This was a private moment, and a tough guy and a tough dog were feeling good together.

Before long, the two of them took off running across the park. It had been raining, and there were puddles every three steps. They were both sending up sprays of exuberance. Near the end of the story, the guy dropped the leash and they ran together, one of the most beautiful sights of a lifetime. Then the dog came back and they walked home to the pound together. That was the last shot on television.

The next day I got a horrendously nasty phone call from someone who complained that the guy had let the dog go free and no one should ever let a vicious dog like that go free and I should be ashamed of myself for putting that on the air and she would be forwarding her complaint to City Hall and asking the mayor to have a close look at this program of allowing dogs at the pound to go out with strangers and run free.

I was glad she called. Before that I had been feeling much too good.

I hadn't been planning to do another story about dog walkers at the pound, but then came Gabriel. Gabriel was a life-stopper, one of those fellows you meet and he becomes part of your life until you die.

I was driving along Raymur Street, about a block from the pound, and there on the sidewalk was a frightening sight. A dog's leash was tangled in the wheel of an electric wheelchair. The young man in the chair was struggling but unable to reach it.

I stopped, and it was obvious I had better do something quickly. The dog was choking, and the expression of the man in the chair was near panic. He said something, but I did not understand it; he had the garbled speech of someone with cerebral palsy. The leash was tight, and I had to lift up the dog and press him against the chair to get enough slack to unhook him. And what did the dog do to say thanks? He growled at me.

Look, I saved you, you ungrateful mutt, I was thinking. But I knew he had to blame someone, and the guy in the chair was his friend.

The guy in the chair said thanks. He struggled with the words but he asked me to hook the leash over the handle of his chair and then he was off. I drove the rest of the way to the pound and told Bob about what had happened.

He was shocked. He kept asking, how was Gabriel?

"Who's Gabriel?" I asked. "The dog?"

"No, the guy," said Bob. "I know the dog. The dog is tough. But I'm worried about Gabe."

Gabriel Gargol was their best dog walker and their most faithful, Bob said. Unless the snow was too deep for a full-sized Hummer, Gabriel showed up every day in his wheelchair. And he wasn't a local resident. No, sir. Gabriel started his daily trips from an apartment house near Georgia and Denman. He drove his wheelchair in sun and heat and rain and cold across the West End, past the gay couples holding hands, along the edge of Skid Row, where the drug dealers were selling crack to young girls, and in and out of Chinatown, where cures for everything could be had. The ride took almost an hour. Why? So that he could walk a dog. Any dog. No fuss, no shaking his head, no saying he didn't want that one. Any dog that needed a walk, Gabe was there to take it for a half-hour stroll alongside his chair.

The folks at the pound usually gave him the middle-sized dogs. Too big, and the dog might end up taking Gabriel for a ride; too small, and the dog could wind up in Gabe's lap, having fun but no exercise.

I did a story about Gabriel, this neat guy without the ability to walk who took dogs with no homes for walks. If it had not been for the accident with the dog that one day, I would not have met him. Nice story. Just another nice story, but then one day, I would learn from Bob, Gabriel did not show up at the pound.

On his way out of the underground garage of his building, which was the way he came and went, he had dropped something just after the metal security gate went up. He leaned over to pick it up, and he leaned too far. His chair tipped over. Gabe fell on the ground, and the gate came down. It landed on his neck. He could not scream. He could not push. He could not get up. He died there and was found later by a driver leaving the garage.

Why didn't the gate go up when it hit something, like it should have? Why did he fall over? His chair was designed so that wouldn't happen. We don't know. We only know that Gabriel was a good guy, and now you too may possibly miss him as much as I do. You may miss him as much as the folks at the pound do and as much as his family does and as his aunt, who goes back to the garage every month on the day he died to put flowers there.

But none of us miss him as much as the dogs do.

ManWoman

One of the strangest men I have ever met, probably one of the strangest on this earth, lives a simple life in Cranbrook, which is right near the Alberta border. Cameraman Ken Chu and I were there looking for unusual life forms, meaning anyone who walks to the beat of a different drummer.

"Go see ManWoman," someone told us.

"Who?"

"ManWoman."

"What's his name?"

"ManWoman."

"What is he like?"

"Wacko, brilliant, defiant, kind, gentle. For starters."

"How will I know him?"

"You won't miss him."

"How can you be sure?"

"I'm sure."

"Where?" we asked someone.

"In there." The person pointed to a knick-knack shop with plates and glasses in the window.

"There?" I did not think anyone in a shop that sold lacy cushions and teacups could be wacko enough to hold our interest, no matter how odd his name.

We walked in and a frail little lady said hello. We asked for ManWoman. She pointed to the back of the shop. Was he being held prisoner? Was he a locked-away hermaphrodite? No one had prepared us. That is part of the ritual in Cranbrook, we would learn. Sometimes tourists come by bus just to look at ManWoman, and they leave with eyes unable to blink. Bikers come to see him and leave feeling inadequate. Neo-Nazis have heard of him and leave with less hatred.

"Can you tell us anything about him?" we asked the little lady.

"Oy vey," she said with a bit of Yiddish mixed with a Rocky Mountain twang. "He's my son and I love him."

We walked into the back room, where we could see a man painting a picture. His back was to us, so all we could see was long hair reaching the collar of a yellow coverall. Then he turned and smiled. Ken and I stopped. I was not going farther.

"Come in," he said.

"No, thank you. We're fine here."

"Don't be afraid."

What we saw was an eye tattooed in the middle of his forehead. Hanging from his ears were swastika earrings. On the backs of his hands were numerous other swastikas, tattooed into the skin. I had seen guys like this before and generally had not invited them home for lunch.

"You're an artist?" I said, trying to say anything other than the obvious, like, why the heck do you have swastikas hanging from your ears and covering your hands? I was afraid if I did ask he might tell me, and the war has been over for a long time.

"Yes, I'm an artist, but you really want to know about the swastikas," he said. "First let me show you something."

I knew Ken was filming this because I could hear the camera going behind me. The next thing ManWoman did was open the buttons of his coverall. Then he turned his back to us and pulled down the top. I knew Ken was still there because I heard him sucking in all the air that was in the room.

My mouth was open. I wanted to speak, but my mouth would not close.

In front of us was a back covered with swastikas: big ones, small ones, fancy ones, plain ones, pointed, blunt and scrolled, ones facing this way and that, and going down below where the coveralls were still guarding his privacy.

"That's a lot of swastikas," I said, being a master of the obvious.

Then he turned around. His sides, chest, stomach, neck and then arms, don't forget the arms, were covered with the most hated symbol in the world.

"Peace be with you," he said.

He was born Patrick Kemball in 1938 in Cranbrook, and he wanted nothing in life other than to be an artist. In his twenties, after a near-fatal car accident, he had a vision from heaven. Others have had similar experiences. When you come close to death you sometimes find a meaning in life, and that meaning sometimes comes from a source and a place that you can only associate with a higher power. He vowed to be God's artist.

Patrick tried, successfully, to be accepted as a Trappist monk at a monastery in Kentucky. But they wanted him to give up his art.

"Give up art? But I am God's artist," he said. So he went back to Cranbrook, studied art at several well-respected schools and began painting pop art pictures of pure joy. He was called a spiritual Andy Warhol. You look at a painting of a boxer, titled *Harmless Boxing Gloves*, or a painting of a woman in a corset, titled *God's Foundation*, and you smile. His work has been bought by many leading galleries and private collectors.

So far, nothing too much out of the ordinary for a person who has found a meaning in life. But then came the dream.

"God told me to revive the good name of the swastika," he explained. "It's a magnificent symbol that had healing powers for thousands of years before the Nazis destroyed it."

So he had one tattooed on his arm.

"Are you a Nazi?" someone asked.

"No, a soldier for God."

After he had done some research, he had an Egyptian-styled swastika tattooed on his other arm.

"Are you sure you're not a Nazi?" people said.

"No, I'm on a mission."

Then came a swastika from the Aztecs, and another from the Hindus, followed by a Buddhist swastika. Each got permanently inked onto his body.

"You must be a Nazi."

"No, I'm an Aztec, a Hindu and a Buddhist."

And more, of course more, because the Vikings, the Greeks, the Romans, the Christians and even the Jews had swastikas. The Jewish ones were found in ancient synagogues next to the Star of David.

"You can't fool me. Anyone with fifty swastikas is a Nazi."

"Afraid not," said Patrick. "I'm a Jew, and a Christian, and a Roman, and a Greek and a Viking."

And he added even more. By the time he ran out of room on his body he had more than two hundred tattoos, all but one of them swastikas. The sole exception was the third eye inked onto his forehead.

Then he did another borderline unusual thing. He felt that women were not getting a fair shake in society, so he changed his name, legally, to ManWoman. At the same time his hair was growing long and his bulk was increasing.

"That does it," said his detractors. "You are a Nazi biker transvestite faggot."

"No," said ManWoman. "I'm a mystic artist poet. I'm not gay, though I laugh a lot."

He showed us pictures of the 1916 women's hockey team from Edmonton. They had swastikas on their sweaters. He told us about a town in Ontario named New Swastika in 1911 because of a lucky gold strike. We saw pictures of swastikas from around the world, all of them predating the Nazis.

Many people have religious experiences, but they usually wind up wearing the symbol of their religion. What ManWoman is doing is much more courageous. He is teaching us to defend what is not currently acceptable. Those who stood up during the civil rights movement were brave. Read *To Kill A Mockingbird*. Those who defend new immigrants who look different, sound different and wear different clothes are brave, and few.

ManWoman stands behind his belief in a way that he cannot escape. He cannot change his mind. When the going gets tough, he cannot suddenly deny he ever believed it. Not this guy. He is not crazy. He is one of the most self-confident people I have ever met. He is a national treasure, but I don't think the government would acknowledge he exists.

If you go to Cranbrook and he offers to roll up his sleeves or show you his back, one warning: take a deep breath before you open your eyes.

Joe the Shoeshine Guy

If you get ten shines from Joe, he will give you one free. Your name is in his little plastic box of index cards. All you have to do is find your card yourself and make a check mark each time you get your shoes shined. Once you have checked off ten, hand the card to him. Presto, a free shine.

But you have to be quick because Joe has got a line-up of customers. Some are wearing thousand-dollar suits and five-hundred-dollar shoes. You are in the underground of the Royal Centre mall, just off Melville Street, where Joe has worked for more than ten years.

Joe is in his fifties. Joe has pictures of famous people who have had their shoes shined by him: Sylvester Stallone, Bob Lenarduzzi, some politicians, some media people. Joe cannot read. Joe cannot count. Joe does not charge GST because he cannot figure out how much it would be. Joe cannot file his customers' cards in his card box because to him the letter A is not much different from the letter Z and you cannot put things in alphabetical order if you do not know the alphabet.

"I did not get much schooling," he says.

That's about all I know of his past. But I have seen him when he has hired those less fortunate than himself who could not get a job anywhere else. He teaches them to shine shoes. I have seen him at Christmas, when he wears a Santa hat and gives half his money to charity. He figures out the amount by pushing half of the money he gets to one side of his shoebox and half to the other.

And I listened to him when he said he loved to sing while he worked but only knew one song, "Hey, Jude." And he only knew one line of that song, the first, in which a sad song is made happy. He would hum and then go back to the line he knew.

After doing a story about him and his song, I went upstairs to Burrard Street and saw some kids in their twenties sitting on the sidewalk with signs saying: "Hungry, Homeless, Please Give."

Their shoes were dirty.

Joe could give them lessons.

Little Fisherman

It was one of the most touching stories of my life. There was just one little part we left out. The scene: Trout Lake in East Vancouver. The character: a nine-year-old boy.

He was fishing, but he was doing it the truly old-fashioned way, with a crooked stick he had found and a string tied to the end. The stick still had some twigs on it.

"Catch anything?" I asked.

"Not yet," he said. He did not take his eyes off his line.

"Is your mother or someone around?" I asked. In our world, you do not speak to a young child without a parent or guardian nearby. In every story we do about a child, we always make sure there's an adult obviously with the kid in one of the scenes, so that everyone knows the child is safe.

"That's Sybil, my foster mother," he said, pointing to a woman sitting nearby reading a book.

We got permission from her to talk with him and take his picture. I was thinking that the boy was awfully young to have a foster mother. Somewhere in his past was a troubled life that we knew nothing of.

He told us his name was Reilly, and then he pulled his line out of the water.

"Sybil showed me how to make the sinker," he said. It was a rock that the string was wrapped around and tied to. Above the sinker was a paper clip, bent like a hook.

"I made that myself," he said proudly. Then he put a piece of hamburger meat on the paper clip and threw the line out, stretching his arm to make it go farther. The string was barely five feet long.

"Ever got a nibble?" I asked.

"No, not really," he sniffed and said. He said he had felt a tug on the line a few times, but it was probably a log or something that snagged the hook.

"Did you think it was a fish, even for a second?" I asked.

He nodded. "It felt good, but just for a second." You could almost see the goosebumps at the thought that maybe, maybe, he did have a fish.

Sybil walked over to us, just to check, which is a very good thing. She told me he fished here almost every day. He had been with her all through the summer and into the fall, and the lake had become his closest friend.

"I don't know if it's the fishing or the water or the quiet," she said, "but after an hour or so here he is very calm."

"Do you ever get tired of not catching anything?" I asked.

He sniffed, and then in words far older than his years, but maybe not than his life, he said, "I think anything is possible when you really, really try to do it."

He did not take his line out of the water while we spoke. He stared at the spot where the string entered the lake. I was standing at his side, crouched over to listen and to hold the microphone. The cameraman was standing alongside me, aiming the lens at the side of his face.

Reilly sniffed again and said, "I think it's possible that I can catch fish, if I keep trying and trying."

Such innocence and faith. He possessed what so many of us spend our lives casting about for and never finding.

But what could I not include?

I wrote this same story for *BC Outdoors Sport Fishing* because it was so touching. I left part of the story out there, too.

All during the interview with this most mature and deep-thinking child, a great glob of green mucus slowly descended from his right nostril. Then he sniffed it back in.

And then he would say something wonderful. And after that the green glob slowly oozed out almost to his upper lip and he sniffed it back up.

I wanted to say, stop. Blow your nose, kid. I can't stand here and watch. Yuck. And here it comes again. And sniff, the glob went up, and then something beautiful came from his heart and his mouth.

It went on and on. It was a very normal thing for a nine-year-old, but impossible for an adult to watch without feeling slightly, okay hugely, ill, and knowing I must tell this kid to blow. But I couldn't. He was concentrating so deeply on the line, and he was giving the world eternally good advice. I could not stop him. But I could not ask any more questions because my stomach was starting to feel too queasy.

That is everything you need to know about life. The most beautiful moment from an angel with a fishing pole, while the glob goes up and down and up and down. Don't even think about it.

The story ended.

"Did you see that?" I asked the cameraman back at his van.

"I saw an incredibly sensitive kid," he said.

"Anything with his nose?"

"Couldn't see his nose," he said.

And so the story on television was heavenly. The runny nose did not turn the beauty into a joke. We are always so close to disaster, and to triumph.

After the story ran, a few people went to the park to offer Reilly new fishing rods.

"No, thank you," he told them. "I will catch fish with my own pole."

It was a good lesson for me. We all have our shortcomings. Just grow up and ignore them.

Liz's Handbag

The Queen came to visit BC a few years ago. Okay, time goes faster as you get older, and maybe it was more than a few years ago. But we noticed when she arrived that she was carrying a handbag. She always carries a handbag. All the time she is saying hello to someone, or to tens of thousands of someones, she has that bag right there in case she needs it.

What's in it, we wondered?

We spent countless hours on the telephone and with researchers and scouring press releases trying to find out its contents. Surely that would not be a royal secret. I have a wife who carries a handbag, and I know that whatever you want, it's in there, even if it can't be found.

While we were trying to uncover this potentially interesting information we decided to go to the street and find out what is in the everyday woman's purse.

The first woman we stopped opened hers and said she had no idea what was in there. She pulled out some underwear.

"Oh my gosh," she said, "this is embarrassing. I changed on my way from my boyfriend's to a job interview."

The second woman said her bag was heavier than a weightlifter's claim to fame. "It's all because of these," she said, and she pulled out a key ring. No, it wasn't a ring; it was a link from a chain that would hold a freighter in place. Those keys weighed five pounds, at least.

"What are they for?" I asked.

"I don't know," she said. "I've had them for years, and I only use two of them."

Women are mysteries.

We met a woman whose purse weighed twenty pounds. If you are into metric, that is more weight than most people are trying to lose by dieting. Carrying it tired her out, she said.

"So why do you?"

"Go out without it?" She looked shocked. "Never."

Another found cookies that she had lost a week earlier. One had an expired telephone calling card.

"That's bright," she said.

Regarding the Queen, it turned out that her press bureau had never been asked the question before.

"We have it on the highest authority that she carries a hanky," they said, "and a camera, gold-plated, lipstick and her glasses."

"Any money?" we asked.

There was a pause.

"Her Majesty does not have a need for money."

Of course not. She owns half the world.

And that reminded me of the best Queen story ever. It happened when I first arrived in Canada, so I did not report on it. I just read about it, with amazement that anyone could be so brilliant.

It was 1973 and Queen Elizabeth was coming to Canada and everyone was buying flowers to give to her. Every flower shop in the country was dying to have a picture taken of the Queen holding their flowers. The trouble was that when the Queen is handed a bouquet, she holds it only for a few seconds before she hands it to an attendant waiting behind her. So the pictures have to be taken very fast.

Florist Thomas Hobbs, in Vancouver, had a bright idea. I had first heard about Thomas Hobbs a few months before, when he got national headlines by doing something many thought was a scandal. At the time, Neil Diamond and Barbra Streisand had just recorded "You Don't Bring Me Flowers." It is a song of love gone off the deep end. In his showroom window in Kerrisdale, a neighbourhood where nothing bad ever happens, Hobbs arranged a mannequin of a woman lying across a bed. She was holding a bunch of roses in her lifeless hand, having obviously done herself in. Since he didn't send her flowers anymore, she got them herself and then killed herself. That would show him.

And did it upset the people of Kerrisdale? Oh my heavens. There was outrage. You could not show such violence or hostility or things like that in public, people said. Hobbs did, and he wound up with stories about him running right across the country. What better advertising could you hope for?

And then came the Queen and Hobbs's little idea. Everyone always gave her bouquets. But when the order came to his shop to make an arrangement for a little girl to give to the Queen, he made—and here is the brilliance—a small decoration of beautiful blooms and blossoms to be worn on the wrist.

Every flower shop in the city was cutting long stems; he cut short. Every other shop was making large; he made small. During every public appearance the Queen made, the crowds were filled with people handing her bouquets of flowers, which she handed to her aide. And then came the moment when the little girl handed the tiny gift to Her Majesty. The Queen graciously thanked her and then slipped the corsage onto her wrist.

For the rest of the afternoon, every picture taken of the Queen had Thomas Hobbs's flowers in it. I still cannot look at a picture of the Queen without thinking how brilliant is one of her flower-loving subjects.

And what did the last woman we stopped on the street for the What's In Your Bag story have in her bag?

"Oh, I forgot about this old flower," she said. She held up the frayed remains of something that had once been bright and colourful. Then she smiled and put it back in her purse. She did not say another word, but I guessed she was remembering something very nice.

One Good Idea

They are all around us. You could pick one out of the air before you finish reading the next sentence. Something that others will want because it is such a good idea, but Lord, you came up with it. You did something with it before anyone else did, and therein lies the genius.

I met Bryan Dyck while he was planting flowers at the base of trees on Main Street. He is a genius.

But I did not see a genius, I only saw someone planting flowers and thought, that's nice, a guy doing something to make the city look better.

"What do you do?" I asked.

"Nothing," he said. "I'm retired."

I feel bad when I hear this from someone who looks my age and I think I am on the Freedom 75 Plan.

"From what?" I ask as I always do.

"From nothing. I retired when I was thirty and haven't worked since then."

I knew I was listening to someone who made genius look like a slow learner. Tell me your story, please.

As he put pansies into the dirt around the roots of trees, I heard what you or I could have done, but Bryan actually did.

About 1973, the government of Canada decided that this would become a metric country. Billboards went up saying that metric was fun. Movies in theatres were preceded by lessons in the metric system. Almost everyone in the country felt their imperial-sized toes were being stepped on.

"I'm not going to learn that metric stuff, it's too hard."

"Metric is a mystery."

"Give me an inch or give me death."

It became difficult to count in Canada. Grocery stores were ordered to sell their goods using metric measurements, though they could post the prices in pounds. As a result, we still have potatoes that can be bought in pounds or kilograms, and kids still don't know if a pound of potatoes is too much or too little. So they leave the shopping to mom and dad and just buy fries instead.

Bryan Dyck said, "What's the problem?" Bryan was a long-haired hippie printer. He was a counterculture guy with beads and tie-dyed shirts who said, "Man, I just want to groove with the times." As far as metric was concerned, he said, "That's cool. That makes sense. It's just ten times ten times ten. Anybody could get that."

Rather than fight metric, he started explaining it to his friends. It was easier than explaining Zen Buddhism or the meaning of Gestalt psychology, both of which were the rage in the early seventies.

"Look, a metre is a hundred centimetres, and a kilometre is a thousand metres. That's not hard."

His friends remained mystified. Walking a kilometre sounded a lot harder than walking a mile.

"We don't like it," they said. "We'll never understand it."

So Bryan went into his little print shop and created a tiny book, fewer than a hundred pages long. On the first page, it said, "Basic Metric in Five Minutes or Less."

He called himself Metric Man, and in the book he used silly pictures of himself. They showed a lean Bryan posing and dancing and pointing to numbers on a blackboard. It was the art of the day. Inside the front cover was a picture of him rushing along holding an attaché case. On the side of the case it said he was "the world's smallest publisher."

First he sold a handful of copies to his friends. Then he got some books into the local bookstores. Soon, because metric was news, the story was picked up by local newspapers and then national ones.

And then somewhere in New York, someone at a television station read a small wire story about Bryan and because metric was just beginning to be talked about in the US, he was invited down for an interview. He wound up on national US television. Within a few weeks he had sold almost a million copies of his book. Since he was both the publisher and the printer, his only overhead was the cost of paper and the ink.

"I never had to work again," he said.

He has spent a lot of time in Hawaii since he retired. Now he plants flowers around trees on Main Street, and he helps young people start businesses, and he has a personal campaign to wipe graffiti off the street. Every time someone puts up a mark, he paints over it. He is a good guy. He has many friends and smiles much of the time.

One simple question I often ask myself, and I will ask you: how did you react when you heard that metric was coming our way? I know what I did. I said, "I'll never understand it." And the next day I went back to work.

The Nod

I t was an exposé that upset many reporters. They had gone to school and completed Reporting 101 and 102, and they knew how to interview and write a simple sentence.

They all worked in television so they had also studied the "Stand Up," the moment in most stories when the reporter stands in front of the camera and says something that could have been much better expressed over a picture of what they are talking about. But in the Stand Up, the reporter gets to be on television and after all that is the main reason to work in television.

"Look, Lucy, there's that fellow who I saw on television. He's famous, you know."

"Why is he famous?" asks Lucy.

"Because he's on television."

"What's his name?"

"I don't remember. But he's famous."

And after mastering the Stand Up, these polished journalists moved to the next level of television reporting: the Nod. That is the all-important moment during an interview when viewers see the face of the reporter and the back of the head of the person who is the subject of the interview. And in most of those shots the reporter is nodding. Sometimes there is a head shake or a look of surprise, but mostly the head is nodding, sort of like a bobblehead on a well-suited body.

The truth is the formal interview is over. But the reporter has asked the subject to stay on just a moment while the cameraman gets some more pictures.

"Just act natural and talk to me," says the reporter.

"What do you want me to talk about?" asks the subject, who has just been interviewed on some significant matter of current importance.

"Anything," says the reporter. "The weather would be fine, or what you had for breakfast this morning."

The subject of the interview then talks and the camera shoots the back of his head and the face of the reporter, which suddenly springs into life. The nod, the jerk at suddenly hearing something amazing, the nod again and the eyes that open wide with surprise.

"Thank you." And this time the interview is really over.

The Nod is used during the editing to cut down what the speaker has said, chopping out major portions and glueing the remaining parts together. This is done to make what the person has said fit into a ninety-second story, along with other pictures and of course the Stand Up, leaving about twenty seconds of interview pulled out of a five-minute chat.

Of course all reporters make sure that the trimmed-down words convey the same meaning as the longer version. But you should never believe totally anything you hear or see or read unless you are there to hear and see it, and even then you may not hear and see everything.

The two most accomplished nodders I ever knew were Harvey Oberfeld and Pamela Martin. Each of them could nod so convincingly you would swear they were glued to the interview. Pamela's eyes would open wide and Harvey would half close one eye and move his head forward in a look of total concentration. Two more sincere reporters you would never find. The only trouble was that the interview was already over.

There are many examples of the Nod, in fact virtually every TV reporter I have ever known, including myself, is sometimes in the story, nodding, agreeing, smiling, frowning. No one just stands there listening. In real life you just listen to someone, you don't nod. But on television, you nod. Watch next time.

My story about the Nod was just an honest attempt to bring truth and information to the world. Most reporters thought I should be fired.

The Shadow Knows

It is always fun to do something different, so that when the story goes on the air the producers look at each other after the first ten seconds and say, "Did you know about that?"

And the assistant producer says, "No, I didn't know. If I knew I would have warned you. But I didn't know."

And the senior producer says, "Do you think it's going to work?"

And the assistant producer shakes his head and says, "Cross your fingers. It's too late now."

It started in a back alley at Main and 14th. John McCarron and I were getting coffee. It was only a year after his daughter had been killed, and he was getting through the days with great pain. But some of us, like John, are smart enough to know that while only time can ease unbearable hurt, laughter can sometimes help too.

It was a sunny day in February, and we were talking about hand shadows. I could make a dog and a bird. I did that against a blue Smithright dumpster in the alley behind the coffee shop.

"Why don't we have a shadow show, like a puppet show?" he said.

"You mean for our story tonight?"

He nodded.

"We'll probably be fired," I said.

He half shrugged. Sometimes in life you don't care about little things.

"Sure, let's try," I said. "If it doesn't work we'll go do some honest work, or at least get another coffee."

I got some paper and scissors from a dollar store and cut out a face. It was a circle with circles for eyes and a smiley mouth and lots of snips at the top to make hair: the universal picture of a girl or woman. Then I cut another circle much like the first, but without hair, the universal picture of a man or boy, even though some men and boys have long hair. Then we cut out some paper tulips, and some grass, and a large circle with points around it for the sun, and the story began.

"One glorious day a girl named Sunshine was walking through the fields under a bright happy sun."

What you saw in shadow on the side of the dumpster was the cut-out of the little girl's happy face: the original Little Miss Sunshine.

"She stopped to smell the flowers."

The cut-out head bent down to sniff the shadows of the tulips.

"And when she looked up there was a bird."

My hands, with thumbs locked together and fingers waving, were flying over the dumpster. No finer bird has ever flown over any dumpster anywhere.

But every story needs conflict.

"Out of the sky came a falling sky snake."

That was the coiled microphone cable, bouncing up and down and threatening Little Miss Sunshine.

"She shrieked. 'Eiiiiiiiii!'"

That part hurt my throat.

"She didn't like sky snakes."

"Woof, woof. She could hear a dog coming." That was my other acting accomplishment. I could make a bird and I could make the shadow of a dog. "Woof, woof. Shadow the dog was coming to the rescue."

The play had an unexpected intermission when someone from one of the restaurants on Main Street came out back and threw a bucket of ugly-looking stuff into the dumpster. It's not easy to get your show to Broadway.

The play resumed with Sunny, the boy, joining Shadow.

"Sunny was Little Miss Sunshine's friend. He told Shadow to go after the snake."

But just as Shadow was about to make the life-saving lunge, a car backed out of a space next to the dumpster and its rear wheel rolled over the other players, who were on the ground. Little Miss Sunshine and the giant sun and the tulips were now covered with gravel and tire tracks.

But the play must go on. "Woof, woof. Shadow bit the sky snake, which jumped back up into the sky and disappeared."

Another interruption. A second guy in an apron from another shop brought out some boxes and tossed them into the dumpster and looked at us like we were very strange creatures to be hanging around a back alley with little paper cut-outs. He didn't take his eyes off us until he was back inside and had closed the door.

The final act of the play was brief. Little Miss Sunshine said to bald-headed Sunny, "You're my hero." And they lived happily ever after.

We ran the whole thing, interruptions and all. When the story ended the senior producer asked, "Did it work?"

"Check Tony's face," said the junior producer.

Tony Parsons sort of tilted his head in mild disbelief and then laughed.

"I knew it would be good," said the producer.

A Rose for Myrtle

What were we going to do? Another day when it was late and we had nothing. If you feel you have been reading that repeatedly in these pages, that is because it happens repeatedly. But renewed desperation seems to bring about renewed effort. The stories are free, so long as you ante up some desperation.

And there, tidying up a late-winter garden was Rick Harrison. He is the gardening supervisor who told me about Raymond the rooster being gay and about the man who sent his wife's ashes off to eternity in the Nine O'Clock Gun. Maybe he would know something.

"Nothing," Rick said. "Let me think. Nope, nothing."

We had turned to leave when I heard, "Oh, yes. It is Wednesday and Myrtle will be coming."

Who was Myrtle? Myrtle was an old-fashioned name. Maybe there was hope.

"It's not new. Myrtle comes every Wednesday in her scooter, just after 2:00 p.m."

I looked at my cell phone because I did not have a watch.

I didn't really just say that, did I? I didn't really look at my cell phone to find out what time it was? When I was young we did not have a phone. I would be home alone sometimes, in an apartment in New York, with no mother, no father, no siblings, no phone, and I was eight years old, and there was nothing unusual about that. When we did get a phone, it had no dial on it. I picked it up once and a woman's voice said, "Number please." I was terrified, so after that I didn't use it.

Now eight-year-olds treat cell phones like chewing gum. Some things in the world do change. Some do not, like the visit of Myrtle.

I check the time, and it is five to two.

"What?" says Rick. He jumps off the ladder he is on while pruning in the rose garden and starts looking around almost frantically. "I didn't know it was so late."

"What are you looking for?"

"A flower," he says. "I've got to find a flower."

But it is February, and there are no flowers. He runs, literally runs, to the gardeners' maintenance yard, which is protected from the wind, and he scrounges through some weeds and finds the winter shoots of something that looks beautiful. He snips them off, then turns and points.

"There they are."

I can see two people, one in a motorized scooter, coming from the West End.

He runs back to the garden in time to intercept them.

We are running to catch up, but he is way ahead of us. By the time we get there we see him handing the shoots to the woman in the scooter.

"For you," he says. She looks up and says, "Thank you."

After Rick gave Myrtle the shoots the pair went on, barely stopping long enough to say, "How are you? Fine. And how are you? Fine."

We watched them go down the garden path, between the black winter beds where roses would later bloom. One woman walking, one in the scooter. I imagined the woman walking was an attendant because she looked very caring. She was almost fifty years younger than the woman in the scooter.

"Every Wednesday at 2:00 p.m.," said Rick. "Unless the weather is worse than awful, she never misses."

And he never missed waiting for her with a flower.

"How did that start?" I asked.

"I don't remember," he said. "She just came by one day and I gave her a flower. After that I couldn't let her down."

I asked how long this has been going on.

"Twenty years," said Rick. "Every Wednesday at 2:00 p.m. for twenty years."

We put the story on television, and it made me feel good.

A week later I got a call from a woman who identified herself as Liz, the woman who had been with Myrtle. She asked for a copy of the story. Myrtle had died. She was six weeks short of her one hundredth birthday.

The next Wednesday Rick pruned the rose garden in silence.

From the phone call, I learned Liz was not a caregiver for Myrtle. She was a friend. I should have known that by the way they interacted, almost as if one knew what the other was going to do or say. But how can you be friends when one person is extremely old and the other is only half that age?

Liz had been too broken-hearted to talk to me that day, but a month later I called her, and I learned I have much to learn about friendship. Most people have friends their own age. That is universal. Friends like that are easy to find. You have things in common and sometimes those friendships last a lifetime, but more often they end when one friend achieves or finds something that the other doesn't have. Friendships where you learn about another at a different stage of life are like links of a chain. One is always ahead, but the two hold together. Links pull us along.

Long before they started coming to the park, Liz cleaned Myrtle's apartment when she needed to make a little extra money. Through that they became friends, and Myrtle taught Liz to play golf on the park's pitch-and-putt course. When Myrtle could no longer walk, the golf days became motorized scooter rides through the rose garden, for twenty years.

Myrtle's obituary in the *Sun* included a long list of relatives. It even talked of how much she had loved her Wednesday outings. But obituaries do not often list friends, and Liz's tears were falling on the paper, not because her name was not there, but because her friend had died. A good friend, especially an old one, is always fresh, like a young flower. And eventually the friendship becomes like a flower you have pressed in the pages of a book. It is always there.

Fly Fishing for Eternity

I fall in love with almost every story I discover. I am not exaggerating. While I am there, the little boy helping his mother shovel snow from their front walk is the most precious sight in my life to me. And when we leave the snowy sidewalk, I say, that is my favourite story. The same for the woman planting a rhododendron that her mother willed to her.

Still, some moments stand alone. It started with a man and his father fly fishing on the grass near Brockton Oval. It looked like a lesson in how to hold a rod, until I watched and listened. After the story was on television, I wrote it again for *BC Outdoors Sport Fishing* magazine. It was the only story I did for them that had no fish in it. It got the most response.

The son's name was David. He stood behind his father, Cliff, gently holding Cliff's arm and guiding him while he moved the fly rod back and forth.

"Keep your arm up high and the line will fly," David said.

Cliff followed his son's instructions, then looked back to see if his son's face acknowledged that he was doing it right.

"Put the line in the air and make it fly," David whispered in his father's ear. "You can do it."

As I talked to them, I learned that long ago David had stood in front of his father, who had told him to keep his arm up and then wave the line back and forth. David had fished with his father since he was a small boy. They fished in rivers and lakes and the ocean. But when David became a teenager, a time when many kids break free of the love of their families and do stupid things, Cliff introduced his son to fly fishing.

Fly fishing is not like throwing a line into the water and hoping you get a bite. Fly fishing is an art, it is poetry with your arm and a hook that is halfway across the stream from where you are standing. It is tying some feathers onto the hook to make it look like an insect and then sending the fly floating over the water and letting it land so gently the fish will think it is a meal settling above them.

Fly fishing kept David fascinated through his teens and young adulthood. Then the years went by, and David had his own family. He became a father, and because of that he spent less time with his own father.

David did not notice the change at first. His mother just said that his father was getting older. Sometimes Cliff forgot where he was going. It was a joke at the beginning. He forgot the punchlines of funny stories. Then he forgot the subject of conversations. Then he forgot his wife's birthday, then his own birthday. Then he forgot his son's name.

That is when David took his father to Stanley Park and stood behind him, holding his arm and helping him to cast a line high in the sky.

"I don't remember this," his father said. He dropped the rod on the ground. "I can't remember. Did I ever do this? I don't remember."

David picked up the rod and put it back in his father's hand, then held his arm until the line was dancing through the air.

"You can do it," said David, the same words that his father had said to him.

They moved the rod back and forth, and the line made a giant S in the air. The father looked at it in amazement, like it was the first time.

"You're a natural," said David. "You can do anything."

The two of them made the line go so high it seemed to float just under the clouds. Two arms fishing with one rod, and the son teaching the father what the father had taught the son. The line moved light as a feather in flight, pulling them together.

You could have sworn that line was remembering how to fly.

The Big Blow

The wind came out of nowhere. Of course that's silly to say, even though I said it in a story on TV. It didn't come out of nowhere; it came from the Wicked Witch of the West, and even if you say it was just nature doing it, well, nature can be pretty wicked. Nature acted like a witch that day.

The wind was a rip-roaring miserable blow, the likes of which had not been seen for forty-five years, which was the last time the miserable witch came through. Typhoon Freda was more devastating, but there was little television coverage, and so it seemed to be a lesser disaster.

Truth is a blending of what happened and what we know about it and how we know it. In 1962 there were only black-and-white, 16 mm film cameras, and the blown-down trees got a few seconds during a fifteen-minute newscast. It was revolutionary. It was fantastic to see trees on TV, or to see anything, but the emotion was as thin as the emulsion on the film stock.

There were newspaper stories about Typhoon Freda, but they concentrated mostly on the numbers and facts. The black-and-white newspaper photos were powerful, but there were only a handful of them.

In truth, the damage forty-five years ago in Stanley Park was greater than the recent devastation. The destruction was so great that the area where the miniature train is now was levelled. That is *why* there is a miniature train now. And the picnic ground nearby was a forest before the typhoon.

But I was not comparing when the Witch of 2006 first swished her broom over the forest. I was ducking. Every reporter and photographer in the city was doing stories on the trees. But no matter how hard we tried, no one could capture with a camera or in words the feeling you had while standing in the midst of a family of mutilated giants.

Turn here, turn there. Wherever you looked you could only say, "Wow. What a shame."

All of us did stories on the scale and the cost and the timetable for cleaning up the mess, but none of them came close to communicating what was there. *Maclean's* did a story so that the nation could read about thousands of trees coming down, but they included only one picture of one tree right near the entrance to the park. It looked strange, but not sad. Cameramen at the site stood in silence, eyes wide and mouths open. It was more than could be gathered in a picture.

It was not as if a city had been bombed. It was not death. It was not another case of human cruelty to men or women or children. It was just a storm in a park, but it was one heck of a storm.

I was doing a story about the forest being heavily logged between 1860 and 1880, before it was a park. The stumps are still there and they, of course, had survived the latest assault. They only survived, I wanted to say, because they are the stubby remains of dead trees. Many have been dead for 140 years.

But how was I going to make that into a story? I had old pictures of loggers standing on springboards chopping away at four-hundred-year-old mammoths. Can you imagine how hard that must have been, to stand on a board not wide enough to hold the whole bottom of your boot and balance yourself while you swung a two-headed axe into wood that fought back at every chop? And then imagine pulling a saw back and forth while your feet wiggled on that board.

The loggers were not allowed to cut at the bottom of the trees because the centre of a cedar is often soft, sometimes hollow, and the straw bosses didn't want that useless wood. So you climb up onto a board eight or ten feet off the ground, come on, you're a man, aren't you, stop your complaining, everybody stands up there, and if you fall off you just gather up your broken body and climb back up and cut. It didn't matter how much wood was left behind or wasted because there was so much more of it.

But I had done that story of logging history before, and there was nothing new in it except the broken trees from the latest wind. Many of them were hemlocks, since it was the cedars that had been logged.

Ken Chu, the cameraman, and I finished with the story. We have been through so much together. We were treed by a grizzly bear near Bella Coola (see my first book), and we discovered ManWoman together. Now we had finished probably our one-thousandth story as a team. We were done with the stumps and I was not happy because who cares about stumps, and he put away his camera in the back of the van.

"Let's go," I said. "I'll buy you a coffee."

And then the wind picked up. It came out of nowhere. We were just past Prospect Point, and the wind was bending the trees above our heads. They were groaning as only a tree that is taller than a ten-storey building can groan. The hemlocks were whipping their heads like teenage girls dancing to hot rock.

"Maybe you should take some pictures," I said.

Ken looked at me with that dumbfounded look that all humans have when they hear something stupid.

"Maybe we should move somewhere safe," he said, looking around at the hundreds of trees within steps of us that have already crashed to the ground in the heavy winds a few days earlier.

But he had started to unbuckle his camera from the back seat when we both heard a crack louder than thunder right above our heads. We looked up to see a tree being attacked without mercy, and we heard *cracccckkkk*. The wind was pounding it, and it broke and slammed into the ground. There was no hesitation. No yelling "timber" and watching it slowly fall. It came down like a giant hammer just across the road from us. We later learned that the wind was well over a hundred kilometres an hour, and so we guessed the tree went down at about the same speed.

"Maybe we should not be here," said Ken.

I agreed, but oh, did I want these pictures. I looked up, and the few remaining trees right over our heads were bending. No, they were not bending. They were leaning halfway over, and we were under them.

"Just shoot a few seconds and we'll get out of here," I said, but Ken couldn't hear me because the wind was too loud.

He started shooting the trees overhead and I saw a CBC satellite truck passing us. It was white and large and the only markings were CBC on the side and it was ten seconds past us when I heard a tree cracking. I shouted. What did I shout? I have no idea, but on the tape all you can hear is "Keeennnnnnnnnnnnn!!!!"

Ken turned just in time to catch the breaking of a one-hundred-foot hemlock and the crashing of its ten tons of wood across the satellite dish on the top of the truck. The truck got squished down like something that should not squish as the tree hit the heavy steel-reinforced cage that protects the massive amount of electronics inside.

The tree broke in half and the truck bounced back up. The driver must have said some really bad words, I would have, and then with a prayer something like "Holy Bleep, get me out of here," he stomped on the gas and kept going.

The time on the videotape between the sound of the crack and the hitting of the truck was forty-five frames, one and a half seconds. If the truck had been slower, don't even think how much slower, if it had been a snap of the fingers slower, the tree would have hit the cab, which is not reinforced.

"Did you get it? Did you get it?" I shouted to Ken.

"I think so."

It was something that photographers spend a lifetime waiting for.

He rewound the tape and looked through the viewfinder. "I got it!"

"I'll buy you a large coffee. Let's get out of here."

The story I wrote in a Global truck parked on Hornby Street just off Georgia, with the wind howling and the light so dim inside I had to stand up and hold my notebook in close to the ceiling light, was not about the history of logging, but about the ghosts of the old trees, the stumps. The hemlocks that had been spared a century earlier were now going down. The ghosts of the cedars spoke through the wind, and disaster happened right before our eyes. It was a spooky, dramatic, frightening story, and it worked fine.

The editors at the TV station called for Ken's shot, which was then sent to them by microwave. It would wind up in the opening of the show and in the lead story as well as in mine. In that truck on Hornby Street a bunch of guys, editors and reporters and cameramen, stood looking at the shot like it was a goal scored in hockey. Then Randene Neil, the noon anchor who was also doing a story about the windstorm, stepped into the van. She saw the picture and asked, "How is the driver?"

We all looked at each other. That was a question no guy had asked. I suddenly felt very small.

The bottom line: Everything that happens, every story of every bit of life, has uncountable ways of being told. No matter what you see, someone else may come along with clearer vision.

You Look Wonderful

The miniature horse was one of my favourite storm stories, but not because of the horse. Sure, the horse was as adorable as only a miniature horse can be while it is being walked around like a puppy dog by two young women in the snow in the park. It was a week after the storm, which had left no stories except those of devastation.

"We walk Brandi every day," said Shirley. "That's Brandi with an i."

She and Elizabeth work in the children's zoo at Stanley Park and once a day they take fourteen-year-old Brandi out for a gallop or a trot or a walk, depending on Brandi's wishes. No one rides Brandi. She was born in the zoo and named by a *Province* photographer who took a picture of her the spring day she came into the world.

The photographer needed a name to put in the caption, and by the time he got around to remembering that he had forgotten to ask the name, everyone at the zoo had gone home. So he made one up. Okay, you are right, journalists are scoundrels. But it sounded like a nice horse name and if they wanted to change it, fine. It was only engraved in newsprint, not in stone, he thought.

Wrong. Stone can wear away in time. Newspapers get saved. "It has been Brandi, with an i," Shirley proudly said, "ever since."

"Would the two of you move together and walk her for a moment, so

I can do the promo that says you two will be coming up at the end of the show?" I asked.

"Do I have to?" asked Elizabeth.

During the filming of the story she had not exactly been hiding, but she had not been easy to see. She was there talking about Brandi and scratching Brandi's neck and being helpful, but then I realized every time I talked to her she was on the other side of the horse.

"I don't want anyone to see me," she said.

"Are you hiding from the taxman?" I asked.

She looked at me like I was stupid and understood nothing.

"It's these clothes," she said, tugging at her sweatshirt. It was grey and had some dirt from the farmyard on it. She also had on baggy sweatpants. "I look terrible."

Oh, my goodness, I was thinking. She can't quit now. I mean, she can if she wants to. I can't force anyone to be on TV. But on the other hand, how am I going to talk about an upcoming story of two women walking a miniature horse in the park if you can see only one woman?

"You look wonderful," I said.

"I look awful."

"No, you look good."

"No, I don't."

I was looking at a very pretty woman who looked extra sexy in loose-fitting farm-girl clothes, and she was worried. I didn't understand.

"You're such a girl," I said, not knowing what else to say.

"And if a guy sees me like this, what is he going to think?"

"I think he'll think nice thoughts."

"You don't know anything," she said.

This went on for forty-five seconds, during which time you can get in a lot of "I look terribles", countered by many "You look wonderfuls."

In the end she relented, so long as they walked way over there and the camera stayed way over here.

When the story ran we included all the "I look terribles," and the "You look wonderfuls."

Over the next week I got a hundred comments about the story, almost all of them like the one from the cashier in the supermarket I go to.

"We laughed and laughed. That young girl was so funny; she should be on television with her own show."

Almost no one mentioned the horse.

The Christmas Tree

As much as I love the people who take care of Vancouver's parks, there was one little incident that ticked me off. Rules and regulations were put ahead of heart and common sense.

In 1995 a cameraman and I were wandering around Third Beach when we saw two women decorating a small tree at the far end of the parking lot.

"What'cha doing?" we asked.

"Decorating a tree," they said.

I like simple questions and simple, direct, honest answers. Can you imagine if that question had been asked of a politician?

"I am initiating a program to alter the landscape for the benefit of constituents who may be parking here, so that they will appreciate me and my government. That is my tree. I raised the money for it. Do you have the spelling of my name? Those are my pictures surrounding the tree. Is that microphone on?"

Nope. Sharon and Gladys were just decorating a tree. They didn't say anything else.

Gladys was older, probably in her seventies. She was a retired teacher from England, which sometimes produces odd people. She wore red tennis shoes.

"Why are you wearing red tennis shoes?" I asked.

"I like them," she said.

Sharon was maybe fifteen or twenty years younger than Gladys and still working as an optometrist. They went for walks and had tea, as friends do. Then one Christmas they decided to do something else, to decorate a tree in Stanley Park. They decorated trees on the other side of the park, around the miniature train, to raise money for burn victims. Why not one other small tree way over here, they thought.

When we met them, they were hanging up a few shiny garlands and some plastic non-breakable decorations, but mostly they were hanging up small freezer baggies. They didn't say they were doing that; they didn't say, "Look at us, look what we are doing." They just did it.

"What are those?" I asked.

"Christmas presents for homeless people in the park," they said.

Inside the bags were dry, brand-new gloves and socks.

So nice.

We did a story about Gladys and Sharon and it ran that night and everyone felt good. But the next day, somewhere in the office of the administrators of the park, there was a meeting.

We were not there, but I believe the meeting went something like this:

"Did you see what those two women were doing? Do they have a permit to do it? Isn't that a violation of some obscure regulation designed to keep people from doing things like that?"

It took three days for orders to come down from the office of the supervisors to the staff who actually go into the park. The next thing I knew I got a call from Sharon.

"They took the decorations off our tree."

So the women went back and put up new garlands and balls and more bags with socks and gloves. It was only a few days before Christmas, and by the time the grinches returned a second time the bags were all gone, presumably to people who were happy to get a gift for Christmas.

The next year Gladys and Sharon were back with more decorations and more bags of socks and gloves. Their tree got decorated, and the park officials took the decorations down.

The third year I got another call from Sharon. Gladys had died, she told me, but Sharon and her family were going to carry on the tradition. They decorated the same tree with garlands and socks and gloves, and this time they left a picture of Gladys in the branches. The socks and gloves disappeared on the first night. The park workers took the rest of the decorations down and left them on the ground, apparently a little afraid of the ghost of Christmas past.

Sharon called to tell me, and we did a story about the battle between the angels and Scrooge. The next week the tree was cut down and removed.

Mostly the people who run the parks are wonderful. But sometimes rules and regulations are like vines that grow too tight and choke the beauty out of things.

The Old Man and the Squirrel

I wanted to pretend I was Ernest Hemingway, but I could not afford to get to Africa. Instead I was on East 7th Avenue, just off Victoria Drive.

Cameraman Mike Louie wanted to show me a tiny house that was being built. It was just over eleven feet wide, barely three and a half steps across, and that was on the outside. Inside, when you added the walls, it must have been hard to pace the floor.

But there was a problem: no one was home, no one was building, no one was squeezed inside. In short, no one was there to tell us this was the greatest way of living, or to explain this was an experiment in minimalist living, or to lament that this was ridiculous. On television you need someone to say something, especially something extreme: the best, the worst, the narrowest.

We turned around to leave and went through a time warp. Suddenly, we had stepped into the wilds of the African Savannah and encountered the eternal struggle of life and death. Meaning, a cat was stalking a squirrel.

But it was not just a cat, it was a wily white predator. And it was not just a squirrel, it was a pitiful, warm-blooded creature that probably had children at home waiting for their mother. You've got to have the good and the bad, or you have no story.

It was the world Ernest Hemingway had made famous and made a fortune from. So I wanted to write:

The white cat took a step. The cat stopped. It sniffed the dead, dry air.

The head of the grey squirrel jerked, then froze. It drew a bead on the puff of killing white fur armed with claws.

The street was a still life of coiled steel.

It reminded me [this is still Hemingway writing] of the bottle of cheap homemade wine Pierre and I shared during the war in a back room of a sleazy Moroccan café where the rice was cold but the woman behind the veil was hot. Don't ask me about her.

"Wine?" he asked.

"Yes," I said.

He poured. We drank.

The cat and the squirrel were like that.

"Die," thought the cat.

"No," thought the squirrel.

The meaning of life was in the hunt on 7th Avenue. But Pierre had told me never to spill the beans on the meaning of life.

So I kept quiet.

Of course Hemingway already had that style sewed up, so on television I simply wrote, "The cat is almost getting the squirrel. Oh, no. But look, the calvary is coming to the rescue."

A young mother and three little kids were walking up the street toward the cat and the squirrel. The kids ran to pet the cat, giving the squirrel time to scoot up a tree.

The last pictures Mike took were the way I like all stories to end: the squirrel sat safely on a tree branch looking down, and the cat lay on its back getting its tummy rubbed. What a perfect world.

Except I said "calvary" in the story. Tony Parsons, the astute anchor, commented on it in a patient and understanding way that reminded me of my drill sergeant in basic training when I had the wrong eye open while firing an M-16 on the rifle range.

"You are the stupidest soldier I have seen in my entire life," was the way he put it.

Tony was kinder. "Wrong word" was all he said.

I had had the cat being saved by the hill on which Jesus was crucified, Calvary, instead of by heroic soldiers on horseback, the cavalry.

Hemingway did not have to fear the competition.

Birds in High Places

I couldn't believe this one. The idea came in by telephone because no way would I be able to spot an open balcony door twelve storeys up and see a small bird flying into a condo.

"She's right there," said Janice Reithofer. She pointed at a fig tree in her living room.

The bird was sitting on a branch, a female about the size of a finch, like a canary except not yellow and not serving a life sentence behind bars. She was free and she was chirping, trying to lure the last of this year's offspring out into the wild world, away from indoor heating and television.

"Every year for the last four years," said Janice.

Every year since the time she accidentally left her sliding balcony door open, the bird and its mate have flown in and built a nest on the valance above her drapes.

"Altogether, fifteen babies," she said.

Janice climbed up on a chair and held a mirror over the nest to show us how she kept count of the eggs. Her husband Frank sat in an easy chair, proud of their maternity ward.

"Now we always leave the door open a crack, even if it's cold outside," he said.

How did the mother bird find this spot? It was one of those mysteries of nature that make nature so mysterious.

There are more than six hundred condos in this complex near Metrotown, and somehow, out of all of those identical balcony doors and windows, this bird keeps finding the same one to call home. Maybe she just likes being close to the grandparents.

And while we are on birds, there is another bird story I get called about every year, and every year I tell the callers that I have already done the story three times, but they must have been out enjoying this event instead of watching TV, for which they should be complimented.

The sight is a great black cloud that spreads over the sky between Vancouver and Burnaby every evening from early fall until early spring. The phenomenon also happens in Prince George and Kamloops and basically every city that has crows.

It starts in late August with a trickle of birds, but by September the sky is thick with swarms of shouting, chattering black birds coming from all directions and heading for the Willingdon exit off Highway 1. The birds have another name for their destination: Party Town.

By Christmas there are a quarter of a million crows flying in waves above the traffic on the highway. They come flying in from all over Vancouver and Burnaby and North Vancouver and Coquitlam. Shaughnessy crows mingle with those from Whalley. East Side birds buddy up with pals from Point Grey. On any night it is not storming or sleeting or hailing or snowing you can see them heading for the gathering of the clan. They actually do the same thing in bad weather, but then it is a case of black birds against a black sky, and with rain running down your back it is hard to be a devoted crow-spotter.

They are like the buffalo of old who ran in waves across the midwest, except that the birds are in the sky and they don't look like buffalo.

Crows are supposedly the smartest of all birds, and they have an inborn need to party. So every night of the year when they are not raising a family—in short, right after they kick the last of the kids out of the nest—they fly to the hottest spot in town for crows, which happens to be between the edge of the McDonald's parking lot and the lot for Dick's Lumber at Willingdon and the highway. They talk and mingle and swap stories, probably about what they found in a garbage can or who is not being as monogamous as humans give crows credit for. Go there any night between the end of summer and the beginning of spring, and you will not have to rent the movie *The Birds* to have a Hitchcock kind of experience.

They have been gathering there ever since the area that is now called Still Creek was actually a creek, not a cement-lined culvert, and there was a forest for the birds to nest in. But then some other creatures came along and cut down the trees and replaced them with an industrial park, which is not a park at all.

It is not a bad life cycle: six months of domestic duties and six months of nightclubbing.

They are much smarter than the creatures who drive by below them every weekday morning and night for most of their lives and take two whole weeks off a year to drive somewhere else. Imagine being a crow. Imagine having a party every night. Where did we go wrong?

In Praise of Slugs

When spring comes, the garden shops are filled with things to make other things grow. There are fertilizers and soil enhancers and sprinklers, but piled up high and selling like a true necessity will always be slug killer.

The boxes say "Death to Slugs." Kill them, murder them, slaughter them. Yucky slugs. Disgusting slugs. Slimy, vile slugs. What could be better, I thought to myself, than to offer a tribute to those poor creatures?

So, if you will, picture a slug, in super close-up, sliding across the grass straight toward you. Then imagine soothing classical music, a Bach cello concerto, written almost as if to the pace of a slug. It is playing in the background.

Then the voice: "It is so easy to pay tribute to a flower or a tree, but we think it is also fitting to praise one of nature's garbagemen. Hence, a tribute to a slug.

"If you look at slugs closely they are almost magical. Follow their tentacles, which wave like wheat. It is not so bad to spend an afternoon looking at slugs. They are not so ugly. Okay, they are not that beautiful, either, but if you spent your life as a moving compost bin you might not consider beauty to be a major necessity. They have been around since the dinosaurs but did much better than those lofty, famous creatures. They are still here. There are five thousand types of them. Some have gills for living underwater and some, like the hunk of slime and skin and muscle that is crawling toward your raspberries, have lungs.

"They have overcome the problem of being lonely in life—being ugly might contribute to this problem—by evolving both male and female sex organs in the same body. The male part is near the head, the female near the tail: sort of like in the human species. At night slugs just curl up. They are not running an empire, so they do not worry about inbreeding."

Now a pause. No words. Just the cello music flowing under the slow glide across the grass.

After a moment: "Most gardeners want to kill them. They do eat lettuce and flowers, but they also consume tons of debris and turn it into fertilizer, which helps more flowers and lettuce to grow."

A crescendo of music, then: "It's easy to admire birds or chipmunks. But if you would like a challenge, try slug watching. Just like watching butterflies or petting dogs, it will slow your heartbeat and soothe your thoughts. No medicine, no doctors, no hangovers. Slugs, like cats or bunny rabbits, will make you feel better. You just have to let it happen."

Guinea Pigs at Work

I can only tell you how this couple cuts their grass. I cannot tell you where they do it because what they do is illegal. But it works and it's wonderful.

One half of the couple is Ingrid Rice, who draws editorial cartoons for scores of community newspapers across the country. Editorial cartoonists are among the strangest-thinking people on earth. They take an important concept, turn it into a cartoon and usually make a point about how absurd the whole issue is. But to do this you have to look at life in a way that basically no one else does.

When students were protesting the rise in tuition fees, Ingrid drew a picture that showed a girl with an iPod ($250), designer jeans ($150), fancy sunglasses ($100), a cell phone ($200) and name-brand runners ($200) holding a sign that said "Down with tuition hikes. I can't afford an education." You get the idea. In fact, anyone who saw the cartoon got the idea.

Ingrid's lifelong mate is Bob York, a musician who plays at Rossini's in Kitsilano most nights and can play on the keyboard anything anyone can name. Musicians are also among the strangest-thinking people on earth. They sort of feel their way through life.

What Ingrid and Bob have at home are guinea pigs. Not one or two or three or four. It would be fine if they stopped at six or seven, or eight or nine. Don't ask how many. It's usually over a dozen. That is why I will not tell you where they live because the guinea pig police would descend on their home and there would be a standoff and the next thing you know bylaw officers would be trying to break down their doors and satellite news trucks would be outside and supporters of guinea pig owners would be marching in the street. It is easier not to say where they live.

The guinea pigs live in a towering guinea pig condo in Ingrid and Bob's kitchen, and they're allowed out to run free through plastic plumbing pipes in the living room. As I said, musicians and cartoonists, especially when they are also guinea pig owners, think in strange ways. But the labour-saving device Ingrid and Bob showed us is a work of ingenious art. They have a large backyard. They do not have a lawn mower. In the summer they simply put the guinea pigs out on the grass and cover them with a screen cage about six feet long and four feet wide that has no bottom. The guinea pigs just eat. And then they fertilize the lawn. And when they are finished in one spot, Bob and Ingrid move the cage.

On one beautiful sunny day we watched the couple mowing their lawn. They took out two lawn chairs and mixed some lemonade and opened their newspapers. Not a sound from an engine, not a wisp of exhaust, not a cord to be untangled. They just read and stretched out in the chairs and relaxed as the grass was trimmed.

By the time the guinea pigs have taken care of one end of the yard, the grass at the other end is just starting to need attention. So it is, "Get back to work, you pigs." Draw, make music or eat: it's a tough life for everyone.

Hopscotch

"You've got to come and see it," said the person on the phone. It was a little girl talking.

I hate that. How can I say no to a little girl who has gotten the courage or encouragement to call. I know that the lemonade stand she runs with her friend may be the most wonderful thing in the world to her, but how many lemonade stands can a guy drink from?

Life is a conundrum. Last year I did three stories on lemonade stands and the boss said he would fire me if I did such a thing again. He would not mind if I did three stories on a single-malt Scotch stand, if there was such a thing, and brought him back samples, but lemonade?

"One more and you are out the door," he said.

Slowly, and with my eyes toward the heaven of fluorescent lights overhead, I asked, "What should I come and see?"

"Hopscotch," she said. "We have the world's longest hopscotch."

"Oh, thank you," I whispered.

"What did you say?" she asked.

"I said that sounds very good," but knowing that no one in the world has the world's longest hopscotch. That would be like the world's longest piece of string or the world's longest list of problems, although there is Murphy the

Whiner, who seems to always have things going wrong. But then everyone knows a Murphy the Whiner.

"How long is your hopscotch?" I asked.

"You've got to come and see it," she said again.

What could I do but go and see it. She told me it was on James Street, a quirky place squeezed between the grittiness of Main Street and the lushness of Queen Elizabeth Park.

I arrived like a judge on *Canadian Idol*. Is your hopscotch good enough for the evening news?

The girls came screaming. How was I going to make a reasoned verdict with twenty jumping, yelling under–ten-year-old girls trying to influence me?

"Here, here, look," they said.

I looked, and looked, and I raised my head and kept on looking. Their hopscotch started here and went all the way down the block, then across the street and down the next block.

"And then we go around the corner," they said.

"Lights," I said.

Okay, we didn't need lights. It was daytime, but it is fun to say that.

"Camera."

They started hopping.

"Wait," I said.

"Action. Okay, now you can hop."

And in a line that kept growing as more girls joined in, they hopped and scotched and kept hopping, in squares numbered one to, "What's the end number?" I shouted as far as I could shout.

"We don't know yet," came a relayed reply.

Some girls at the end of the line were chalking down more boxes on the sidewalk even as the other girls were advancing.

They were well past a thousand when disaster invaded. The neighbourhood boys came and got in behind the girls and started hopping and scotching, though they did not have the technique down as good as the girls. Many of them were missing the boxes.

"Don't film them," yelled several girls. "They didn't do anything to help us."

A neighbourhood conflict, just like big people.

"We can do it. It's our street too," said the boys.

"Can*not*. You didn't help," said the girls.

But the boys insisted and kept going, much to the girls' disappointment. But then peace came again to James Street. They were boys, after all, and this was hopscotch, and after a quarter of a block they lost interest and went off to do boy things.

The story ended with the girls hopping along in their endless boxes. Everyone who watched the story was saying, what a lovely neighbourhood. And I know some mothers were out later that evening teaching their daughters the almost lost art of making squares with chalk and then hopping down the road in a game that sometimes has no end.

The Blackberry Test

This is a story about blackberries, and I do not mean those all-consuming hand-held rulers of people's lives. I mean the kind that God invented before someone else put a copyright on the name.

The original variety have good, traditional uses: wine, jam, pies and toppings for ice cream. But I also think they could make the world a better-run place. We could eliminate election fraud and end up with the truly best-qualified to be our leaders if we instituted the Blackberry Test. The test would be given to anyone who wants to be prime minister, or premier, or mayor. In fact, anyone who wants to be in public office, or be a judge or a CEO, could win the position only by undergoing this simple, honest test

First, a verifiable generalization: People who pick blackberries are good people.

Look at their qualities. There is no such thing as a timid blackberry picker. Blackberry pickers are not afraid to stick their arms into thorn-filled brambles. And they have self-control. If they eat them as they pick them they will not have them.

They are humble. They stand in front of a pile of twisted vines laced with thorns, often just off a busy street, while they try to gather one tiny berry at a time. It is not something they flaunt.

They have other attributes. Fortitude, since it takes a long time to fill even a small bucket. Determination: always the best berries are just out of reach. And they are quiet. Blackberry pickers don't chatter. It takes concentration to work your fingers around those thorns, and distractions like gossiping or complaining or bragging are usually followed by a painful jab. Nature does not tolerate distractions.

Now, imagine if politicians were required to pick blackberries to get into office.

We would send them into the bush with just little plastic pails, and while they picked, the first benefit we would notice would be silence. Non-talking politicians giving peace to the electorate. Already we are winners.

There would be no speeches or mud-slinging or impossible platforms. We would watch while they picked, and we would be able to see who has courage and determination, and who can concentrate long enough to get the job done. We would see who uses imagination when they discover that the highest branches have the best berries. Seeing someone turn a coat hanger into a hook shows the person has more problem-solving abilities than simply sending in the military.

We would see who has self-control because the berries are sweet and tempting, just like all those government contracts, and we would learn which pickers can resist nibbling while they are supposed to be working. We could also measure their tenaciousness and bravery, and see who is willing to stretch themselves the furthest, and who is not afraid of appearing awkward or getting scratched while exploring new territory.

It is not the candidate who gives the best speeches or looks the most stylish or makes the most alluring promises, but perhaps the first one to fill the bucket who might just be the best person for the job. And at the very least, they can serve blackberry wine at their victory dinner.

When I did this story on televison, someone called the station and complained that it was dumb. I called him back and asked why. He said picking blackberries proved nothing. What about world politics and taxes and wars? Those were the issues, he said.

What do you need to solve those problems? I asked.

Imagination and courage and new ways of doing things, he said.

Then let's start with blackberries, I said.

Or you could try the yo-yo test. When Mike Harcourt was running for mayor of Vancouver, I asked each of those in the race to show us how they could perform with a yo-yo. Only Mike would do it, and he did it well. The others said playing with a yo-yo was ridiculous.

Mike, of course, won and turned out to be a superb mayor and later premier. The yo-yo knows.

Comfort in a Cone

It was a warm day. That had something to do with it. But it was mostly the excitement.

Remember when the BC ferry lost control of its rudder and then smashed slowly into the pleasure boats at Horseshoe Bay? It was disaster averted. The captain made a brilliant decision to steer away from the dock, a move that saved both the ferry and the dock. Instead he went into the bay, ploughing in slow motion through the tiny pleasure craft, and lodged his ferry in the sand. The accident caused a lot of damage, but the captain avoided tons more.

There were reporters and photographers swarming over the dock and the town, most working cell phones to get in touch with experts and officials who were in offices downtown or in Victoria who were themselves on phones talking to the officials who stood staring at the ship.

"What happened?"

"We don't know."

"When will you know?"

"We don't know when we will know. But we will let you know as soon as we can let you know."

And then the cell phones went back into pockets, with everyone knowing they would be informed or officially misled as soon as something was known.

More people came to look, more officials, more reporters, more passengers getting off other ferries who did not want to leave until they could ask, "What happened?"

To which they were told, "We don't know."

Horseshoe Bay was like Grand Central Station at rush hour. I knew all the angles would be covered except one that I saw staring at me from almost every hand. While one hand held either a cell phone being used to tell others that a ferry had crashed, or a camera recording that a ferry had crashed, the other held an ice cream cone.

It was a summer day. No one had been hurt. No one was screaming on the ship to be saved. It was a quiet disaster. It was the kind where you could hold your kid up on your shoulder and say, "Look. The ferry was supposed to go there, but it went there through all those little boats over there."

And the child would respond with, "Can I have some ice cream?"

So an ice cream cone was bought, and then someone else watching the officials in their hard hats standing on the broken dock talking into their cell phones also bought a cone.

Buying an ice cream cone is infectious, like yawning. Soon most of the people watching were licking ice cream cones, and I could see a story developing based on a soothing premise: ice cream goes well with disaster.

Fifty years before Jesus, the Roman emperor Nero was licking his ice cream inside the coliseum. He had sent some of his slaves into the Alps to gather snow and ice and bring it back to him so he could be coolly sweetened while watching death and destruction.

That was no mean trick, since the Alps were a week of hard running from Rome, plus a couple of days climbing to get to the snow. And Nero always wanted his treats in the summer when the poor slaves had to run down the mountains carrying huge stacks of snow, hoping that they would be able to pass it off to chariots that would race across the country like FedEx on a mission with human organs. When the ice and snow got to Rome it had to be scooped out of leather bags and put into a bowl and covered with fruit juice so that Nero could have his sweet, cold treat while watching the gladiators cut each other to ribbons.

Now ice cream was going well with a ferry disaster, which seemed historically consistent, but here the only pain would be to insurance companies.

I called the office. "I have the ice cream angle on the non-sinking."

"You have the what?"

"The ice cream angle. You know, the sweeter side of the low-tide-no-body-got-hurt slow-motion-disaster-story."

"Someday we're going to fire you."

"Sounds good," I said. "I'll go into the ice cream business and get rich."

I knew Vince Misceo had done the same thing.

Have you been to his house of 508 flavours? It is a rotating selection. Two hundred and eighteen flavours are on sale at any one time, and you can get a free sample of anything or everything. The place is next to the railroad tracks on Venables Street near Raymour, a few blocks west of Clark Drive. In the summertime they are open almost twenty-four hours a day. But I have also done stories there of line-ups in the winter. You can get garlic ice cream (ugh) or twenty types of chocolate (yummy) or thirty kinds of fruit (super yummy) or forgetaboutit. You want it, you imagine it, you dream of it, Vince will have it.

The amazing thing about Vince and his wife, Pina, is not just their ice cream but their success. When I first met them in the early 1980s, they owned a sports bar on Commercial Street, an extension off Commercial Drive. They served food, they had pool tables and a satellite dish the size of Texas, and in the back they made their own ice cream, just a few flavours, just a sideline, a passing thing in case anyone wanted dessert. But they went broke. Their place was far away from the trendy part of Commerical Drive, south of Broadway in an area that is now filled with condos but then no one knew about except a few artists and writers and editors who did not go to sports bars.

Out of money, out of work, what do you do? So many people whine about that and contemplate suicide or, worse yet, borrowing from relatives. Vince didn't. He used what he had. That was his plan. He and Pina rented a booth at the PNE and sold the one thing they knew how to make that did not have a satellite dish or pool table connected with it. They made ice cream. On top of their tiny booth they put a bold sign: "La Casa Gelato, 40 Flavours."

Forty choices in a booth the size of one of their old pool tables. That was gutsy. But the ice cream was good and the customers lined up and they soon had enough money to open a store on the wrong side of the tracks. Actually, there is no right side of the tracks when you are right next to the tracks, and Vince's store is six feet away from the tracks.

But there is a rule in business: Nothing succeeds like good ice cream, no matter where you are. Make something delicious and customers will find you.

If it had been on the wrong side of the tracks, it became the right side, the side with the long line-ups of those wanting ice cream. Freight trains pass literally six steps from the shop's front door. That should be enough to drive away customers, but even at midnight on a summer evening there are sometimes hundreds of folks out on the sidewalk in this industrial neighbourhood licking their 218 flavours and watching the trains.

"Name the flavours," I said to Vince.

"Basil, ginger, carrot-avocado, curry, cranberry, rosemary, twenty kinds of chocolate, garlic . . ."

"Stop. I had your garlic once," I said. "I prefer chocolate."

They get so many customers they had to rent the lot across the street and turn it into a parking lot. I remember Vince saying once long after midnight, "I wish they would go home. I need some sleep."

Articles have been written about La Casa Gelato in Germany and Japan. Vince has the stories on his walls. A writer for an Italian newspaper asked why Vince had to go all the way to a frozen country to make super Italian ice cream. Come home, he said. Vince has been written about in newspapers in New Zealand and Australia. What I like best is the *New York Times* story recommending his tiny ice cream factory as somewhere you must visit when you're in Vancouver.

I drive by the store almost every day and over the years have noticed that when there is a disaster somewhere in the world, locally or internationally, a fire somewhere in the city or a war somewhere in the world, there seem to be more people eating ice cream. It is a way to cope.

Once I did a story at the store on a cold February day. A kid was standing in the slush on the ground with the rain coming down. He was eating ice cream.

"Aren't you cold?" I asked.

He nodded.

"Isn't he cold?" I asked his mother.

She nodded.

"So why are you eating ice cream?" I asked.

"Becaussssseeeeee"—he shivered so much he could hardly say the word—"becausssseee I love iceee creaaaammmmmm."

His tongue reached out for another lick, but his hand was shaking so much that he could not bring the cone and the tongue together.

"I loooovvvvve it," he stammered.

He was a trooper, an ice cream soldier, just like Vince.

Back at the ferry disaster, I had the tape in my hand and a smile in my heart. But something was missing. All those people eating ice cream looked so happy. I walked into the store where they had all been coming out of.

"A chocolate cone, please."

"Sorry," said the clerk. "We're all out."

"Vanilla?"

"Out."

"Strawberry?"

"Out."

"Garlic?"

"Are you kidding?" he said. "You have to go to that place down by the tracks in Vancouver to get that. But if we had it we'd be out of it."

All the stores in Horseshoe Bay were the same.

"I don't know why," said the clerk in the last place I checked. "All of a sudden there was a rush, like the last thing you want before going overboard."

I drove back to the TV station not thinking about the story or the editing or the ferry. I walked into the cafeteria and bought a frozen pre-made ice cream cone and then went into the edit room. The story was written with one hand on the keyboard, the other holding a cone with luscious chocolate dripping over my fingers as I described a kid sitting on her father's shoulders with ice cream on her face looking at the grounded ferry. Like so often, ice cream had restored balance to the day.

The Fence

For reasons I can't explain, I talk about this fence every time somebody asks about my stories. It happened at Trout Lake, as many stories do.

On a street on the south side of the lake a man was painting his picket fence. Have you ever painted a picket fence? It is a pain to paint a picket fence. First one side, then the other side, then the edges on one side, then the edges on the other. And then the parts that you missed.

The painter was Chinese. He was kneeling down with his brush and his can of paint. His back was hurting. His hand was hurting. His legs were hurting. And his mother-in-law was watching.

Have you ever painted when someone is watching, critically watching?

She said something in Chinese.

"What did she say?" I asked.

"She said I missed a spot."

Then he painted some more and she said something else.

"What did she say?" I asked.

"She said I got some paint on the ground."

Then he painted some more and she said something else.

"What this time?"

He looked and smiled and said, "She said I am using too much paint."

I wondered how he could smile, but I figured he was just a good guy.

She looked over his work, then walked to the far end of the fence and then back to him and said something else in Chinese.

I raised my eyebrows in the universal question.

"She said I missed something back there."

He was the eternal man being driven into the earth by the eternal mother-in-law who forever will wonder why her daughter didn't marry a doctor or a lawyer who had the decency to die young.

And then I noticed that all of the tops of the pickets on the gate leading into his yard were sawed off. It looked so uniform I hadn't seen it at first, but now I could see.

"Why are they sawed off?" I asked.

"Because my mother-in-law is not so strong any more, and that makes it easier for her to move the gate."

In that one line and that one moment there was more love, practical love, real love than you will find in all the relationship manuals in the world. He had cut off the top of the fence for the mother-in-law who complained about his work on the bottom of the fence.

Ten thousand more like him and there would be no need for 911 calls, most wars would end, divorces would be rare, and picket fences would be a symbol of peace and happiness.

Another Blue Flame

If you want a story to tell at dinner tonight, look around. You will find it. And everyone sitting at the table, including the fourteen-year-old child who is driving you out of your mind, will stop and say, "How did you know that?"

You will tell everyone at the table how you discovered that amazing story just by walking down the street.

They will never forget it, and the next night at dinner they may have a story for you.